WARSHIPS
OF THE
GREAT WAR ERA

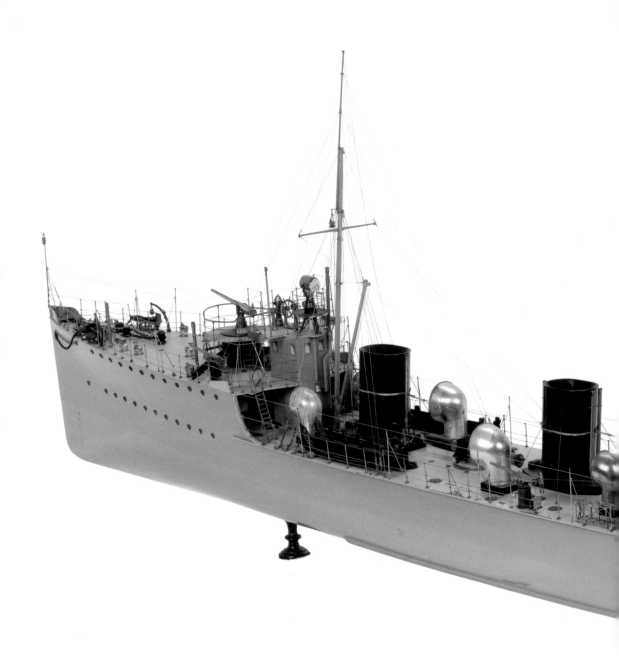

SLR1326 **Half title:** Stern of the armoured cruiser *Leviathan*. The admiral's stern walk – a holdover from the age of sail – suggests a deep-seated traditionalism, but by 1914 the Royal Navy was actively embracing new technology, tactics and methods of command.

SLR0114 **Frontispiece:** The 'River' class destroyer *Boyne*. The development of the destroyer – a shortened form of torpedo-boat destroyer – was essentially a British initiative.

WARSHIPS
OF THE
GREAT WAR ERA

A HISTORY IN SHIP MODELS

DAVID HOBBS

Naval Institute Press
ANNAPOLIS, MARYLAND

Acknowledgements

We would like to thank the staff of the National Maritime Museum's Picture Library, and especially Emma Lefley, who faultlessly organised the complicated issues surrounding the large photo orders. For curatorial help, we are grateful to Simon Stephens.

Other models came from the collection of the Imperial War Museum, the Australian War Memorial and the Australian National Maritime Museum, where Penelope Hyde was particularly helpful.

Individuals who supplied photographs or gave permission to use illustrations of their models deserve particular notice: these are Jim Baumann, John R Haynes, Ian Johnston and Rob Kernaghan. Ian Johnston and John Roberts also kindly helped with the identification of some of the ship's fittings.

References

Models in the National Maritime Museum collection are catalogued by SLR number, and in this book these are quoted at the beginning of each caption to one of these models. Further details of these models can be found on the Museum's Collections website at: **http://collections.rmg.co.uk/collections.html#!csearch;collectionReference=subject-90254;authority=subject-90254**

Searching by SLR number will turn up a full description of the model and any available photographs.

First published in Great Britain in 2014 by
Seaforth Publishing
An imprint of Pen & Sword Books Ltd
47 Church Street, Barnsley
S Yorkshire S70 2AS

www.seaforthpublishing.com
Email info@seaforthpublishing.com

Published and distributed in the United States of America and Canada by the
Naval Institute Press, 291 Wood Road, Annapolis, Maryland 21402-5043
www.nip.org

LOC number 2014943609

ISBN 978 1 59114 190 7

Typeset and designed by Neil Sayer
Printed and bound in China

Contents

1: Introduction

The Royal Navy that mobilised for war in 1914 had just undergone the biggest and most sustained period of technological change in its long history, but its purpose remained unaltered – to secure the use of the world's oceans for British and Allied operations and trade, and to deny their use to the enemy. To achieve this end the Royal Navy commissioned literally thousands of ships ranging in size and capability from the world's most powerful battleship, *Queen Elizabeth*, to high-speed

HMS *Dreadnought*, the battleship that gave its name to a naval revolution, in a finely detailed model by Jim Baumann.

H.M.S. DREADNOUGHT 1907

coastal motor boats, and took up large numbers of vessels from trade. In order to fully understand the war at sea, a knowledge of the ships themselves is vital. Their capabilities, limitations and ability to send, receive or make full use of communications were the biggest influence on their actual, rather than intended, use by commanders of flotillas, squadrons and fleets. The National Maritime Museum at Greenwich has a collection of ship models that includes many depicting ships from the First World War and these provide a unique way of studying the construction, armament, deck fittings and appearance of the actual ships that they portray. The full-hull models allow the underwater features – propeller shafts, rudder and machinery inlets – to be studied and every model gives the observer the chance to examine the whole ship in perspective: to choose a vantage point and study detail in a way that is not possible with a photograph or technical drawing. Now that almost all of these ships no longer exist, models give the only means of three-dimensional inspection available to us. Large and impressive as the National Maritime Museum's collection is, it does have a few gaps, however, especially with regard to submarines, and these have been filled by illustrations from the collections of the Australian National Maritime Museum in Sydney and the Imperial War Museum in London, along with a few top-quality examples by contemporary modellers. Whilst this book focuses on ships operated by the

Royal Navy, the opportunity has been taken to include, for comparison, models in the Greenwich collection that depict both warships built in the United Kingdom for foreign navies and the ships of the opposing German Navy.

In 1914 no British Admiral had ever commanded a cohesive naval force the size of the Grand Fleet or tried to control its movements from a single bridge. Some of the problems had solutions which were known and understood but they had not been practised sufficiently and their implementation in actual operations left a great deal to be desired. Wireless gave the Admiralty the opportunity to direct operations at sea but the responsibilities and requirements of such intervention were not fully comprehended until late in the war. Aviation demonstrated increasing importance as the war progressed and developed from the attempted strike on a Zeppelin base by seaplanes from converted merchant ships on Christmas Day 1914 to the planned air strike with torpedoes on the German fleet in its harbours by aircraft from the world's first carrier by the time of the Armistice in 1918. Other new weapons, including torpedoes, mines, submarines, torpedo-boat destroyers, airships, aircraft and the attendant vessels to maintain and operate them, had to be understood and used to best advantage and their models in the following pages illustrate them in a novel and fascinating way. Even the more familiar weapons such as guns had undergone radical

SLR0029 Of the hundreds of ships that served in the wartime Grand Fleet the sole survivor is the light cruiser *Caroline*, preserved as a Royal Naval Reserve drill ship at Belfast. This is the builder's model of the ship, showing her appearance as completed in 1914.

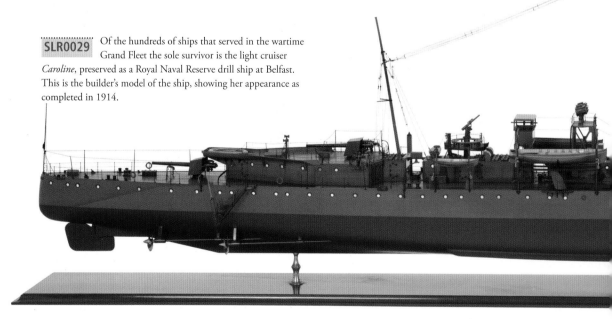

development with greatly increased shell weights, longer ranges and centralised fire-control systems that made accurate long-range fire possible. The need for a damage control organisation to keep ships afloat and in action was understood but insufficient priority had been given to its study in peacetime and in consequence there was not enough training for sailors and their officers. Turbine machinery made unprecedented speeds possible during action and necessitated split-second decisions instead of the hours often available during a sailing battle. Amidst all this new technology, however, manoeuvring instructions by the commander-in-chief were still ordered by flag signals with which the sailors of Nelson's navy would have been quite familiar. The amount of sea covered by the Grand Fleet and the reduced visibility caused by funnel smoke from coal-burning ships and North Sea mist meant that remote ships did not always see flag hoists immediately despite keeping telescopes trained on the flagship. Ships downwind or upwind of the flag hoist could not see them when they were end-on. Signals were always repeated 'along the line' but the time taken for the last ship to acknowledge was often prodigious. Semaphore could be used to signal ships in close company but was of little value communicating with ships at any distance and none at all in the smoke and confusion of a battle.

Throughout the First World War, battleships remained the final arbiters of sea power but the day-to-day work of patrolling the seas and making use of them for the British and Allied cause was undertaken by a range of smaller, specialised ships. Among them were the cruisers, destroyers, submarines, patrol vessels, minelayers, minesweepers, gunboats and auxiliaries described in the following pages. In each case I have provided a description of the model itself together with a description of the real ship it portrays and its historical significance. In each chapter I have spoken briefly about the development of the various types of ship so that the models can be set in their due place and their armament, rig and machinery can add to an understanding of sea warfare between 1914 and 1918. As well as the photographs of the full models, a number of detailed images of specific items of armament or design have been included to give a better understanding of their significance. The further I got into examining these outstanding models, the more fascinating I found the subject. They really do give clarity and a unique understanding of a number of ships that played such an important part in the British Empire's war effort a century ago.

David Hobbs
Crail
April 2014

2: Battleships

Such had been the pace of change in the nineteenth century that by the 1880s fleets were made up with ships of very different designs, armament and capabilities. Standardisation came with Sir William White's *Royal Sovereign* class, so powerfully armed and armoured that only another battleship could oppose them. The principal armament comprised four 13.5-inch guns, two of which were mounted in each of two barbettes, one forward and one aft; these were armoured structures that contained the handling arrangements for ammunition and cordite supply. These were fixed and only the guns themselves rotated but they had to be trained fore and aft at a fixed elevation to be reloaded and the gun's crew were exposed to enemy fire in action. The secondary armament comprised ten 6-inch quick-firing guns intended to pour rapid fire into an opponent. The slower firing heavy guns were designed to smash though the enemy ship's armoured hull to sink it once it had been disabled. Action was expected to take place at close quarters with battle-practice ranges as close as 2000 yards considered normal in the 1890s and ramming was regarded as a viable tactic. All British battleships were fitted with four submerged tubes able to fire 18-inch torpedoes on the beam and it was the threat of enemy torpedoes that caused longer-range gunfire to be developed so that in battle ships might remain outside their range. Smaller 14-inch torpedoes were also carried to arm steam picket boats for attacks against enemy ships in harbour.

Machinery comprised eight coal-fired boilers which delivered steam to two sets of vertical, triple-expansion engines delivering 13,360 horsepower on two shafts for a maximum speed of 18 knots; 1450 tons of coal could be stowed, giving a theoretical radius of action of 4720 nautical miles at 10 knots. There were four boiler rooms, each with two boilers; the forward boilers had their exhaust trunking aft and the after boilers had their trunking forward so that their exhaust was taken out through the two athwartship funnels. The armoured belt along the side of the hull was 18 inches thick, tapering to 14 at the extremities with 16-inch bulkheads. The deck above

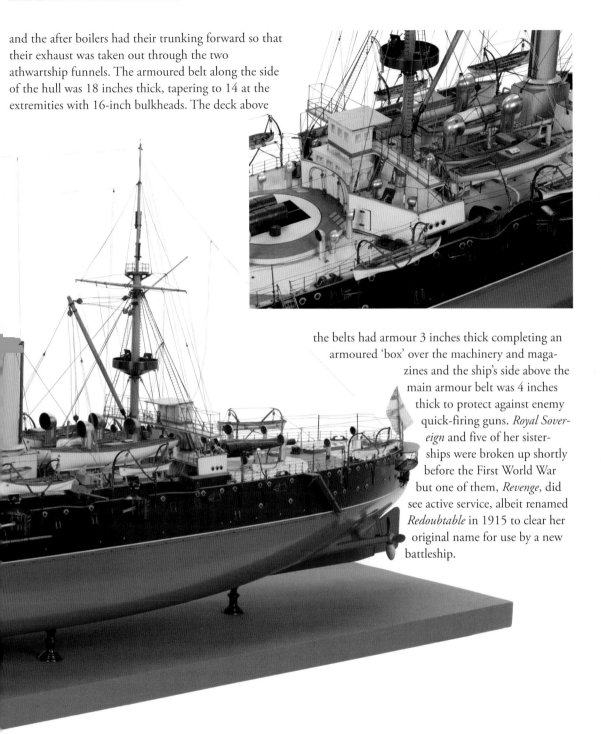

the belts had armour 3 inches thick completing an armoured 'box' over the machinery and magazines and the ship's side above the main armour belt was 4 inches thick to protect against enemy quick-firing guns. *Royal Sovereign* and five of her sister-ships were broken up shortly before the First World War but one of them, *Revenge*, did see active service, albeit renamed *Redoubtable* in 1915 to clear her original name for use by a new battleship.

SLR0117 This superbly detailed 1/48 scale model of the *Royal Sovereign* class ship *Ramillies* was made for her builder, J G Thompson Limited of Clydebank, and shows her as she appeared when completed in 1893. The rigging is carefully reproduced to show the yards and halyards used to hoist flag signals. Note the boats stowed amidships, as clear as possible from gun blast, and the derricks used to hoist them outboard. She had the distinction of being the first British battleship to have steel, rather than iron, armour plating. The model shows the high freeboard which gave this class better sea-keeping qualities than earlier battleships. Note the large fighting tops on both fore and main masts with their machine-guns intended to rake enemy decks with fire and the conspicuous ram bow below the waterline. *Ramillies* served as flagship of the Mediterranean Fleet from 1893 to 1903; with the Home Fleet in reserve until 1911 and she was scrapped in 1913.

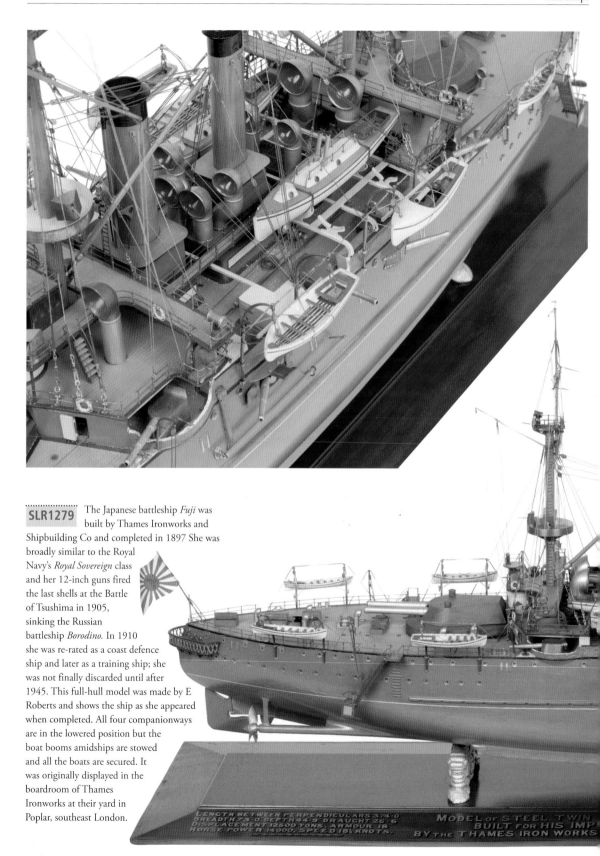

SLR1279 The Japanese battleship *Fuji* was built by Thames Ironworks and Shipbuilding Co and completed in 1897 She was broadly similar to the Royal Navy's *Royal Sovereign* class and her 12-inch guns fired the last shells at the Battle of Tsushima in 1905, sinking the Russian battleship *Borodino*. In 1910 she was re-rated as a coast defence ship and later as a training ship; she was not finally discarded until after 1945. This full-hull model was made by E Roberts and shows the ship as she appeared when completed. All four companionways are in the lowered position but the boat booms amidships are stowed and all the boats are secured. It was originally displayed in the boardroom of Thames Ironworks at their yard in Poplar, southeast London.

Pre-dreadnoughts

In March 1902 *King Edward VII*, the first of a class of eight battleships, was laid down in Devonport Dockyard. They had a main armament of four 12-inch guns in two turrets and introduced a new secondary battery of four 9.2-inch guns in single mountings. A tertiary battery of ten 6-inch guns remained in an armoured citadel making these ships the ultimate expression of Sir William White's basic battleship design. The mixed batteries were intended to 'smother' an enemy with hits but as ranges increased it became difficult to spot which splash came from which gun. The 12-inch guns rotated on armoured barbettes with the breeches enclosed within an armoured shield, by then referred to as a turret. These had become sophisticated structures built by specialised armament manufacturers and were capable of being reloaded on any bearing. These ships were fitted with twin balanced rudders which gave them a tight turning circle but made them difficult to steer on a steady course, earning the class the nickname of 'the wobbly eight'.

The *Lord Nelson* class were the last British battleships built before the revolutionary *Dreadnought* and, like their predecessors, they had a main armament of four 12-inch guns in two twin mountings. The secondary armament, however, was increased to ten 9.2-inch guns in four twin and two single turrets, which led them to be called semi-dreadnoughts. Twenty-four quick-firing 12-pounder guns were mounted as a defence against torpedo boats. *Lord Nelson* and *Agamemnon* were not completed until 1908 and both served in the English Channel at the outbreak of war but went on to see action in the Gallipoli Campaign and in the eastern Mediterranean until 1918. The Turkish armistice was signed in *Agamemnon* in 1918.

Lord Nelson was discarded and scrapped in 1920 but *Agamemnon* had an interesting post-war career, stripped of all armament and used as an unmanned radio-controlled target ship for gunnery exercises between 1923 and 1926 when she was replaced by *Centurion*.

SLR1349 This waterline model was made by the marine artist Alma Claude Cull to portray the *King Edward VII* class battleship *Hindustan* as she appeared while serving with the 3rd Battle Squadron in 1913. It is well detailed with steam pinnaces, cutters and other large boats stowed aft of the funnels and sea-boats on their davits positioned on either side of the quarterdeck and abreast the funnels. A stern walk can be seen right aft, opening from the admiral's day-cabin under the quarterdeck and eleven steel booms can be seen along the hull, stowed aft and upwards from their attachment points with rolled-up steel netting at their ends. These were anti-torpedo nets, which were lowered into the water on the extended booms when the ship was at anchor. They proved ineffective and were removed in 1916. Above the nets, there are two horizontal boat booms which were turned out at right angles to the hull when at anchor so that the ship's boats could be secured to them.

The ships of this class had five Babcock & Wilcox boilers arranged in such a way that the funnels could be fitted fore and aft. By July 1905 when *Hindustan* was completed all battleships had been fitted with wireless telegraphy (W/T) and the high attachment point for the aerials can be seen at the top of the main mast.

Message-handling using wireless was slow, however, and tactical signalling continued to rely on flag hoists similar to those of Nelson's era. Funnel smoke and winds that made flags appear end-on could obscure flag hoists and the problem of controlling formations of warships in unprecedented numbers at high speed was not solved until after the war. *Hindustan* was built by John Brown at Clydebank and served in the 3rd Battle Squadron until February 1918 when she was used as a depot ship for the Zeebrugge and Ostend raids. In May she collided with the destroyer *Wrestler* after which she was not repaired but reduced to reserve. She was sold for scrap in 1921.

EARLY EXPERIMENTS WITH AVIATION
Some of the RN's earliest experiments with naval aviation took place in ships of the *King Edward VII* class. *Africa* was fitted with a wooden platform over the forecastle from which Commander C R Samson RN took off in a Short biplane on 10 January 1912, the first naval officer ever to fly from a ship. Later, *Hibernia* was fitted with a similar platform and Samson took off in the same aeroplane on 2 May 1912 while the ship was underway off Portland; the first time in history that an aircraft had taken off from a ship under way at sea.

This 1/700 model of *Hibernia*'s flight deck was made from the Combrig kit by Rob Kernaghan and shows how the wooden flight deck hampered the forward turret.

SLR1369 This typical shipbuilder's 1/48 half-block model of the period shows *Lord Nelson*'s starboard hull and gun mountings but the bridge, masts and funnels are truncated and not shown in any detail. The hull does, however, show the retention of a prominent ram forward and her balanced rudder aft. The bilge keel was a relatively new feature which reduced the amount of roll and made these ships better gun platforms. The grey area above the waterline is marked with the positions of scuttles, the blank area amidships showing where the 12-inch armoured belt protected the machinery and magazines behind it.

The Dreadnought revolution

The battleship *Dreadnought* was laid down in Portsmouth Dockyard on 2 October 1905, launched by His Majesty King Edward VII on 10 February 1906 and completed for trials on 3 October 1906. Designed under the leadership of Sir Phillip Watts, the Director of Naval Construction, she represented such a great advance in design and capability that all the battleships that followed her in every navy were known, generically, as 'dreadnoughts'. She was the first battleship to have an all-big-gun armament with ten 12-inch guns in five twin mountings, and the first to have turbine machinery; on completion she was the fastest and most powerful battleship afloat. Her BVII mountings

and 12-inch 45-calibre guns were actually ordered for the *Lord Nelson* class but were transferred to *Dreadnought* to speed her completion, one reason why the earlier ships were so much delayed. The turrets were arranged with three on the centreline and one on either side of the superstructure so that up to eight guns could be fired on either beam and potentially six ahead or astern, although the effect of blast from guns fired with their muzzles so near the superstructure was damaging. *Dreadnought* had a large battery of quick-firing 12-pounder guns mounted on the turret roofs for use against torpedo boats. She also had submerged torpedo tubes with four on the beam and one firing astern.

H.M.S. DI

The ship was conceived by Admiral Fisher, First Sea Lord between 1904 and 1910, and rendered all previous battleship designs obsolete. Since Britain had the world's largest battle fleet there were some who criticised the new ship as an unnecessary gamble that meant starting afresh to build up a new lead. What such critics failed to take into account, however, was Fisher's carefully balanced judgement that the Russian fleet had been neutralised in the recent Russo-Japanese War and, since all-big-gun development was likely to be inevitable, Great Britain had seized the ideal opportunity to lead the revolution and use its enormous shipbuilding capacity to its own advantage. The construction of *Dreadnought* in only a year and a day shocked the naval world and there can be no doubt that it gave the Royal Navy a huge psychological advantage. She cost £1,783,883 to build.

In August 1914 *Dreadnought* was the flagship of the Grand Fleet's 4th Battle Squadron but her big moment came on 18 March 1915 when, no longer a flagship, she was returning to Cromarty after exercises with other battleships when *Marlborough* reported sighting a U-boat and a torpedo was seen passing astern of *Neptune*. *Dreadnought's* captain increased speed and steered directly at the U-boat, crashing into it with her ram and causing it to sink rapidly with all hands, but not before its pennant number, *U 29*, was seen clearly. *Dreadnought* was refitting when the Battle of Jutland was fought in May 1916 and, ironically, she left the Grand Fleet in July, considered by then to be too slow to maintain the speed now expected of the fleet. She spent the remainder of the war as flagship of the 3rd Battle Squadron, comprising ships of the *King Edward VII* class, based at Sheerness. By 1918 she was obsolescent and paid off into reserve in 1919. She was sold for scrap in 1922.

This superb 1/350 scale model of *Dreadnought* is not part of the National Maritime Museum collection but was built by Jim Baumann based on a Steel Navy/Rhino Models kit. It deservedly won the Gold Medal as the best in its class at the 2000 UK IPMS National Awards. It shows the ship in outstanding detail and the various boats are worthy models in their own right. There are scale figures on deck and the rigging, bridge ladders and the 12-pounder guns on the turret roofs all show up better on this three-dimensional model than they would on a black and white photograph. Note the sighting hoods on the turret roofs; these were intended to allow the guns to be laid in local control but proved a drawback in action since they provided a vertical surface to detonate the fuses of enemy shells that might otherwise have only grazed the sloping turret roof. Jellicoe had insisted on them when, as a captain, he was Director of Naval Ordnance.

The 13.5-inch gun

Battleship design evolved rapidly through several distinct classes after 1906. The *Orion* class of 1909 introduced the new Mark V 13.5-inch 45-calibre gun. They were fitted in five twin mountings on the centreline with superfiring turrets in 'B' and 'X' positions to keep the required ship's length within manageable proportions. Even then the barbettes for the superfiring turrets raised the design's centre of gravity, which had to be compensated for by an increased beam, which in turn required a commensurate increase in length to maintain speed. *Conqueror,* one of the four ships of this class, was the first ship to have her main armament built for the RN

by the new Coventry Ordnance Works. The total cost of her construction was £1,860,648. By 1909 new 'heater' torpedo designs were achieving greater ranges and the torpedo boats that carried them had increased in size and speed. To counter this new threat, the *Orion*s were fitted with sixteen 4-inch 50-calibre guns which had greater destructive effect than the 12-pounders (3-inch) fitted in earlier classes and could engage their fleeting targets at greater ranges. The arrangement of the main armament had the advantage that all ten guns could be fired on either beam, although only four could be fired directly ahead or astern. The armour plate required to protect the turret

roofs had become a significant aspect of battleship design by this stage since they constituted about 18 per cent of the ship's horizontal surface area and a hit that penetrated the roof could create a flash or fire that could travel down the ammunition supply route to the magazines and shell rooms below the armoured deck.

SLR1401 A 1/48 scale model of *Conqueror* made by her builder, W Beardmore of Dalmuir, showing her as she appeared when completed in 1912. The port side shows the anti-torpedo nets in their stowed position but two gangways are shown rigged. Like some of the early British dreadnoughts, the fore mast was placed aft of the fore funnel and noxious exhaust gases from the boilers often made the spotting top uninhabitable. The surprising reason for this unfortunate choice of location was to provide an anchor point for the boat derrick. Later classes had a more practical arrangement that placed more emphasis on gunnery control than boat-handling and put the fore mast forward of the fore funnel where smoke contamination was less likely when the ship was moving at speed. Night fighting was thought to involve too great a risk since it gave a numerically weaker opponent the chance of scoring lucky hits on the British battle line, leaving the outcome of any battle too much to chance, but the *Orion* class had two groups of small searchlights; one can be seen near the bridge and one aft, just forward of 'X' turret.

The model's rig shows wireless aerials rigged from the bow to the top of the fore mast and then down to the stub main mast. Wireless was an important aspect of communications in 1914 but was not yet fast enough to be used for tactical work. Messages had to be taken from the compass platform to the bridge wireless office and coded before transmission, a process that could take at least twenty minutes even for a short message. The reverse process had to be undergone in the receiving ship with the result that a message could take up to an hour to travel from bridge to bridge. For this reason, the Grand Fleet continued to be manoeuvred by flag signals, backed up by semaphore. *Conqueror* fought at Jutland where she sustained no damage or casualties. After the war she was removed from the operational fleet under the terms of the Washington Naval Treaty and sold for scrap in 1922.

Super-dreadnoughts

The four ships of the *King George V* class in 1910 were logical developments of the *Orion*s. In turn they were followed by the four ships of the *Iron Duke* class in the 1911 programme. These retained the 13.5-inch main armament in five centreline turrets but mounted a secondary armament of twelve 6-inch 45-calibre guns, reflecting contemporary fears about the growing threat from torpedo boats and destroyers. Unlike in earlier British battleships, these weapons were not intended for use against other battleships. There were concerns, however, that these larger guns with shells that weighed 110lbs, considered to be the largest that could be practically worked by hand, were not capable of sufficiently rapid fire to be effective against the fleeting, fast-moving targets that might be expected in an attack by enemy destroyers. *Iron Duke* was the first British battleship to be fitted with an anti-aircraft armament when two 3-inch high-angle guns were fitted in 1914. The *Iron Duke*s were the last British battleships to burn coal in their boilers, although combustion was enriched by spraying fuel oil into the furnaces, and the last to be completed with anti-torpedo nets. At full load they carried 3250 tons of coal and 1050 tons of furnace fuel oil. Eighteen Babcock & Wilcox boilers and turbine machinery developed 29,000 shaft horsepower giving a maximum speed of just over 21 knots.

Iron Duke famously fought at Jutland in May 1916 as the flagship of Admiral Sir John Jellicoe, firing 90 rounds from her main armament but suffering no damage or casualties. After Sir David Beatty became Commander-in-Chief of the Grand Fleet, *Iron Duke* became a private ship in the 2nd Battle Squadron. After the war she saw action against the Bolsheviks in the Black Sea before returning to the Atlantic Fleet in 1926. In 1931 she became a training ship, with her armament reduced, her armoured conning tower, main armoured belt and torpedo tubes removed. In 1939 she became a depot ship in Scapa Flow, moored off Long Hope, but in October 1939 she was damaged by air attack and had to be bottomed in shallow water but continued in service. There was no further role for her after 1945 and she was repaired sufficiently to be raised and sold for scrap in 1946.

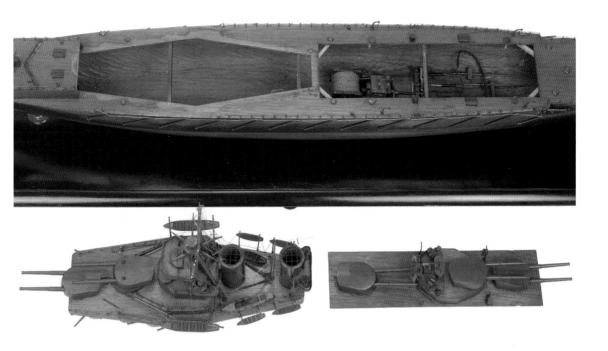

SLR1402 *Iron Duke* was one of the most iconic warships of the First World War and this 1/96 scale model was made by Alfred Graham & Co. Several sections of its deck can be removed to reveal wiring and electrics inside the hull which was, unusually, carved from a single, solid piece of wood. Much of the original interior equipment is, unfortunately, now lost but the connections to the four propeller shafts indicate that the model was originally capable of floating and propelling itself through the water. The model's superstructure and guns are made of metal and show detail but the model is not rigged. *Iron Duke* was built in Portsmouth

Dockyard and took just over two years to complete. Between 1914 and 1916 she flew the flag of Admiral Sir John Jellicoe, the Commander-in-Chief Grand Fleet. The armoured conning tower from which the ship was controlled in action is conspicuous just aft of 'B' turret and the fore mast is located forward of the forward funnel where it was clear of smoke except when there was a strong wind from directly astern. The long ranges at which the main armament could engage the enemy made it necessary to introduce director-controlled firing and the main armament director is visible on the roof of the spotting top on the fore mast above the bridge.

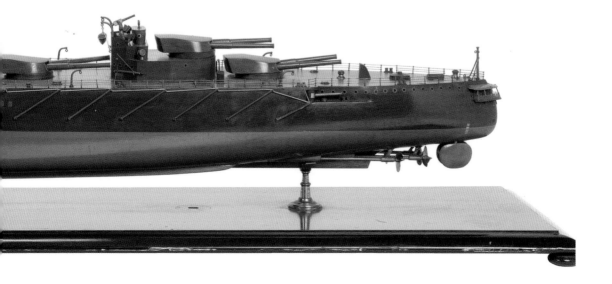

SLR1403 This beautifully detailed 1/256 scale model of *Iron Duke*, formerly in the collection of the Royal United Services Institute, shows her as she was in 1918 with the anti-torpedo nets removed. Carley rafts with neatly stowed paddles are fitted below the bridge and on the after superstructure and the fourteen ship's boats are stowed in the space between the funnels where they were relatively clear of blast from the main armament. The model shows detail changes to *Iron Duke* which indicate the progress made since the outbreak of war, including the enlarged bank of searchlights either side of the after funnel. By 1918 the Royal Navy had evolved its tactics and the Grand Fleet was able and willing to fight a night action if necessary. An enlarged rangefinder is mounted on top of the conning tower to help with long-range gunnery and both 'B' and 'Y' turrets have been painted black with bearing markings in white. These were adopted by the Grand Fleet to help concentrated gunfire when one ship saw a target but others could not. By noting the bearing on which the firing ship's turrets were trained, other ships could train on the same bearing and range could be read off indicators, which looked rather like clock faces, fitted on the bridge facing forward and on the after superstructure facing aft. The 6-inch guns in their casemates are conspicuous in the sides of the raised forecastle deck between the forward turrets and the bridge. The sea-boats abreast the bridge to port and starboard are shown ready to be lowered quickly but held firmly in place by smart, white-painted gripes.

SLR1406 A section of *Iron Duke's* sister-ship *Marlborough* that was originally used as an instructional aid for teaching basic gunnery and seamanship. The hull is made of solid wood with the detail of the tripod fore mast, bridge structure, funnels, 6-inch battery and main armament turrets built up in metal. All eighteen of the ship's boats, including a steam picket boat stowed to starboard, are shown in their correct positions and the derrick that lifted them, together with its kingpost, are correctly rigged. Halyards for signal flags are accurately rigged from the signal deck below the bridge and wireless telegraphy aerials are correctly portrayed. The main turrets revolve, although the guns themselves do not elevate. Red and white lines have been painted on the section and, together with the gun turrets, these are marked and numbered so that various compartments can be identified. The main armament director on the spotting top is conspicuous, as is the rangefinder mounted at the rear of the bridge.

Marlborough herself was built in Devonport Dockyard and completed in June 1914. Like other British battleships she was a wet ship in heavy seas because of the low forecastle but she was a steady and effective gun platform. At Jutland she flew the flag of Vice Admiral Sir Cecil Burney, the Flag Officer 1st Battle Squadron and Second-in-Command of the Grand Fleet. During the battle, she was hit by a German torpedo amidships but was able to maintain station at 17 knots, however, and remained in action, listing to starboard, for a time before being ordered to the Tyne under escort for repairs which took three months to complete. After the war she saw action in the Black Sea against Bolshevik forces but was withdrawn from service after 1929 under the terms of the Washington Naval Treaty. She was sold for scrap in 1932.

THE 15-INCH GUN

The highly successful *Queen Elizabeth* class was originally to comprise four ships but a fifth was added as a gift from the Federated Malay States. They were the first battleships to be built with a main armament of 15-inch 42-calibre Mark 1 guns, two in each of four mountings. This was the best big gun ever designed and used by the Royal Navy. Each gun weighed 97 tons and fired a projectile that weighed 2000lbs with 50 per cent greater explosive effect than the earlier 13.5-inch shell. The hydraulically operated breech mechanism and the rapid loading cage for each gun were new designs, allowing six rounds to be fired in five minutes. These bigger guns allowed a reduction to four twin mountings and the space occupied by 'Q' turret in earlier designs was used for more powerful machinery that gave the class a speed of 24 knots, which was unprecedented for a battleship and close to the designed speed of the early battlecruisers.

They were the first British battleships to burn furnace fuel oil rather than coal. It had a higher calorific value and made refuelling considerably easier but there were concerns at the time that it might not be as easy to procure as domestically produced coal. Tanks built into the ships' double bottom structure were capable of holding 3400 tons of fuel oil but, surprisingly in hindsight, *Queen Elizabeth* and her sister-ships still had to embark 100 tons of coal to fire the galley ranges for cooking.

Queen Elizabeth served initially in the Dardanelles campaign, engaging Turkish forts across the Peninsula from the Aegean by using aircraft to spot her fall of shot. She became Admiral Sir David Beatty's Grand Fleet flagship in February 1917 and was present at the surrender of the German High Sea Fleet in 1918. Her subsequent service in the Atlantic, Mediterranean, Home and Eastern Fleets would fill many pages and she became a household name throughout the UK and the Commonwealth during her long and successful career. She was completely and expensively modernised on two occasions to maintain her effectiveness and was not finally discarded until February 1948 after thirty-three years' service as, arguably, the outstanding battleship of her generation.

SLR1414 *Queen Elizabeth* is shown in this 1/192 waterline model as she appeared after her first reconstruction in 1925-27. Made by Norman Ough, this beautifully detailed model forms part of a realistic diorama which also includes the post-war destroyer *Cygnet*, an Admiralty steam drifter and an admiral's barge. She is moored to buoys at bow and stern and the battery of large searchlights clustered by the funnel shows an improvement in night-fighting capability that would not be bettered until the invention of radar. Her rigging, including the wireless telegraphy aerials, is neatly portrayed. Norman Ough was an outstanding modelmaker whose work was exhibited at the 1935 Wembley Exhibition and he also worked for the Imperial War Museum for a while. Totally dedicated to his craft, it was not unknown for him to have to be taken into hospital suffering from malnutrition because he was concentrating so intently on the model in hand that he literally forgot to eat.

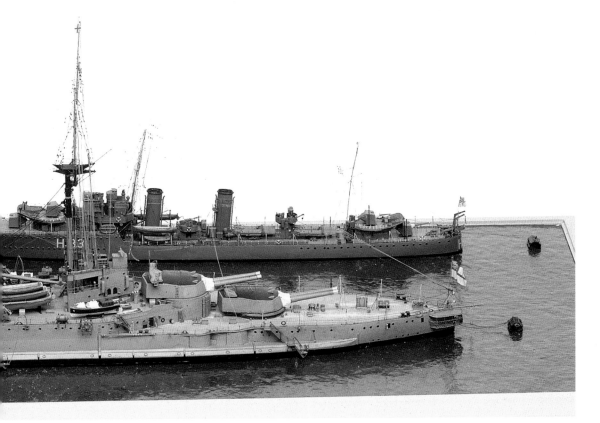

BATTLESHIP SUPERSTRUCTURE

This 1/48 scale builder's model of the battleship *Barham*, made in John Brown's own model shop, is particularly well detailed, so is a good representation of the topside fitting out of a Great War battleship. The model is in the Scottish Maritime Museum at Irvine; photos by courtesy of Ian Johnston.

The spotting top mounted over the 'starfish' on the fore mast. It has a director mounted on top and a brass steaming light mounted on its forward face. The light has a halyard with which it can be lowered to the deck for refuelling or maintenance.

Starboard side details of *Barham*'s bridge structure. Note the two separate locations for starboard navigation lights and the mechanical semaphore arm by the lower one. This was the signal deck from which flags were bent onto halyards for hoisting to the yardarms and six can be seen secured to the cleats at the rear of the deck.

The after superstructure showing two 36-inch searchlights, one on either side of the attachment point for the wireless telegraphy aerial, and a single 24-inch searchlight on a platform on the main mast. Boats are stowed forward of this structure, clear of gun blast, with a derrick secured to the mast. Scuttles in the bulkhead even have gutters over them and the two hatches appear realistically clipped shut. (David Kirkpatrick, by courtesy of Ian Johnston)

The rear of the compass platform showing the 6-inch directors, cylindrical objects with brass-framed windows, to port and starboard, and a 24-inch searchlight mounted centrally facing forward. Painted canvas 'dodgers' would have been fitted to the compass platform guardrails in service to give some protection against the wind. Rigging is particularly well modelled and shows signal halyards, bracing wires and wireless telegraphy aerial feeds. There is a mechanical semaphore arm mounted just forward of the searchlight.

Barham's starboard side amidships showing both funnels and a 32-foot cutter turned out on radial davits with their gripes in place. More boats are stowed on deck aft of the after funnel. The starboard 3-inch anti-aircraft gun is mounted by the boats stowed to starboard of the fore funnel.

The upper part of *Barham*'s bridge structure showing the open and exposed compass platform with its binnacle projected forward over the charthouse and the 36-inch searchlight on the platform under the compass platform.

The compass platform and its equipment. The magnetic compass binnacle is conspicuous at the forward end and the object that looks like a vertical roller at the port side aft is the gyro compass repeater. The rectangular brass devices to port and starboard with what look like clock faces are Evershed bearing indicators and the brass object at the rear of the platform is a clock. The structure immediately under the compass platform is a charthouse and the small hut with the wooden door is described as a weatherproof shelter.

This view of *Barham*'s model shows the port after side of the bridge structure and the rear of 'B' turret with its 30-foot rangefinder. There is a 36-inch searchlight on the platform on the port tripod leg and the port rear side of the conning tower can be seen forward of the bridge. The main armament director with its 15-foot rangefinder is mounted on top of it. The visible part of the bridge structure contains a charthouse and sea cabins. The forward four port 6-inch guns can be seen in their casemates and on the upper deck there is a 3-inch anti-aircraft gun on a high-angle mounting. A whaler is secured inside a cutter with both lashed down onto the deck; ropes are stowed neatly on drums and there are derrick booms secured to the bulkhead. Note the 'butterfly' nuts securing the hatch covers, which are particularly realistic.

The 'R' class battleships of the 1913 programme lacked the speed of the *Queen Elizabeth* class but mounted the same number of 15-inch guns and had a similar 6-inch secondary battery. They were sturdy and effective, if unspectacular ships that continued to give good service into the Second World War.

SLR1427 This model of *Revenge* is made to approximately 1/400 scale and has several inaccuracies but it does have the merit that it was made by Chief Petty Officer Vernon Miles while he was serving in the ship, continuing a long tradition of ship-modelmaking by sailors. Sadly, he was subsequently killed in action in *Hood* in May 1941. The hull is made of wood and the superstructure of brass, paper and other materials that were available to him on board. She was the ninth ship to bear this famous name, which dates back to 1577, and was built by Vickers and completed in March 1916. They were the first battleships to be built with anti-torpedo bulge protection and the last to have the secondary armament in batteries; the latter feature can be seen but since it is a waterline model mounted on a base-board, the former cannot. The larger spotting top with the director on its roof and the rangefinders fitted to the director on top of the conning tower and main armament turrets show the increasing importance of long-range fire control for the main armament. The model shows several traditional features such as the admiral's stern walk right aft and scuttles in the ship's side in the accommodation areas; the area with no scuttles amidships shows where the main armoured belt was fitted. This was 13 inches thick amidships, tapering to 6 inches forward and 4 inches aft with 6-inch bulkheads. Horizontal armour between 1 and 2 inches thick was built into the forecastle, upper, main and lower decks; the main gun turrets were up to 13 inches thick and the barbettes that supported them up to 10 inches thick. In all, armour plate amounted to about 30 per cent of the ship's total displacement of 31,200 tons at deep load.

Revenge served at Jutland and Vice Admiral Sir Cecil Burney transferred his flag to her when *Marlborough* was torpedoed. From November 1916 she was the flagship of Admiral Madden who became Second-in-Command of the Grand Fleet. After 1919 she served with the Atlantic, Mediterranean and Home Fleets. From 1939 she was used to give heavy cover to Atlantic convoys against the threat of surface raiders and in October 1940 she bombarded German positions in Cherbourg at a range of 15,700 yards. She served with the Eastern Fleet throughout 1942 and in February 1943 she escorted the Australian Division from Suez back to Australia. She returned to the UK to pay off in late 1943 and from 1944 she formed part of the Stokers' training establishment *Imperieuse* at Devonport with her sister-ship *Resolution*. She was finally sold for scrap in 1949.

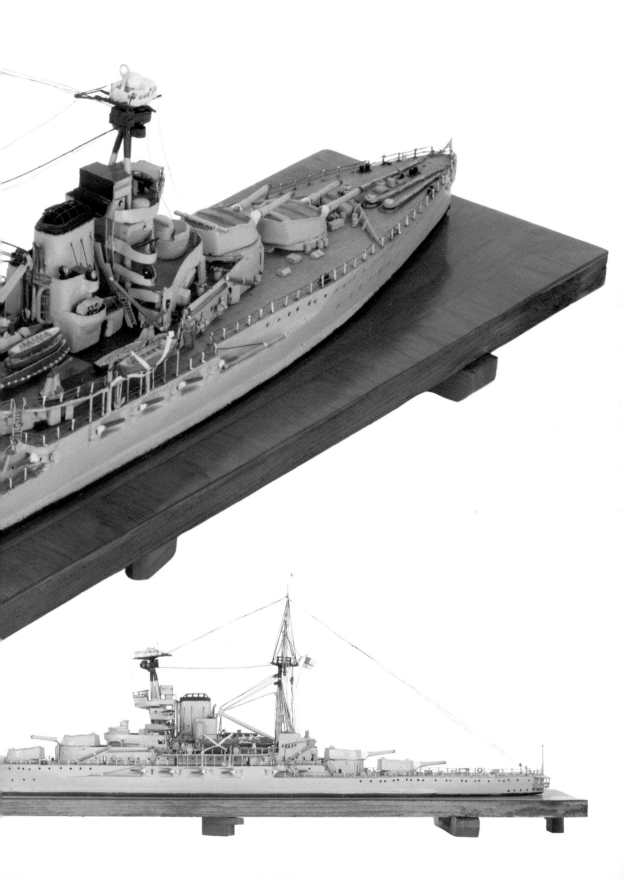

An Enemy Battleship Compared

The German battleship *Baden* was similar, in several respects, to the British *Queen Elizabeth* class, including a main armament of eight 15-inch guns in four twin turrets, but her coal-burning boilers were obsolescent by 1918 and would have limited her effectiveness in action. Launched in 1915, she was the last German battleship to be completed in the First World War and was the flagship of the High Sea Fleet in 1918. After the German surrender she was interned in Scapa Flow and scuttled in 1919. She was subsequently raised and taken to Portsmouth where she was examined in detail by British naval architects. These found that, while her four continuous longitudinal bulkheads allowed for very complete subdivision, the transverse bulkheads were pierced by a number of doors, voice-pipes, sluice valves, pipes and ventilation trunks that would have rendered them far from watertight and reduced their efficiency, with the result that underwater damage would have led to slow flooding similar to that which led to the loss of *Audacious* in 1914. Also, the maximum elevation of the 15-inch guns was only 16 degrees, which limited their range to only 22,000 yards. Firing rates would have been slowed by the time needed to move shells and charges from remote shell rooms and magazines. After examining her, the Royal Navy used her for two sets of extensive gunnery and bombing tests with live ammunition. After completion of the second set of trials, she was scuttled in the Hurd Deep west of the Channel Islands in August 1921. The most important conclusion drawn from the tests was that multiple layers of thin armour plate were useless against large-calibre shells and, as a result, the Royal Navy adopted a single layer of thick armour in its first post-war battleships, the *Nelson* class.

SLR1425 This 1/100 scale builder's model, made by F Schichau in Danzig, was presented to the National Maritime Museum by the War Trophies Committee in 1945 and shows *Baden* as she was when completed. Unlike British battleships, the anti-torpedo nets have been retained and they are depicted in the stowed position. Companionways are in the lowered position on the port and starboard side of the quarterdeck. Another aspect of design where she differed from her British contemporaries was a machinery layout with three, rather than four shafts. While this reduced the weight of equipment and the number of men needed to man it, it was less resilient after action damage and less flexible. Between the two World Wars German naval architects had very little opportunity to create new battleship designs and the eventual design adopted for *Bismarck* lent heavily on the experience gained with *Baden*. The similarity is particularly evident in the appearance of the 15-inch gun turrets.

THE UNDERWATER DANGER

By 1914 it was well understood that the principle threat to the Royal Navy's dominance of the seas would come from below the surface. A single well-placed hit below the waterline might sink the largest ship, and much thought was given to countering the danger posed by both mine and torpedo.

THREAT

Moored Mines

SLR2964 Moored sea mines became a serious threat from the early twentieth century and forced battle fleets to operate outside shallow waters until they had been effectively swept. This model shows a mine and its sinker on the rails from which it would be dropped. The battleship *Audacious,* only completed in 1913, sank after striking a German mine similar to this one. Moored mines could only be laid in relatively shallow, coastal waters and both sides' mines were supposed to be fitted with a trigger which would destroy them if they broke free from their moorings. They did not always work as intended; mines on the surface were always treated as dangerous and detonated by rifle-fire. The model represents a typical British moored mine on its sinker trolley ready for laying. The sphere on top was buoyant and contained, typically, about 300lb of guncotton. It was laid simply by rolling the trolley along rails over the stern of a minelayer; when the sinker touched bottom it acted as an anchor and released a cable drawn out by the mine's buoyancy. The length of cable could be adjusted to set the depth at which the mine would float below the surface but that would vary with the state of the tide and the current: with little current the cable would tend to be vertical; with a strong current the mine was pulled with it to an angle, effectively lowering its depth. This type of mine was triggered by the spikes visible on its sides, known as Herz Horns. These were made of soft metal surrounding electrolyte in glass containers. When a target impacted the horn, it bent, breaking the glass within and allowing the electrolyte to flow into a battery,

Torpedo

SLR2961 A model of a British Mark V torpedo of 1910 made at the Royal Navy's torpedo school in Portsmouth. Both the weapon and its handling trolley are accurately portrayed in copper, silver, phosphor-bronze and brass and mounted on a wooden base. Torpedoes could be launched from a variety of surface warships, submarines, ships' boats and, from 1914, aircraft, to deadly effect. Torpedoes were made for the Royal Navy by the Royal Gun Factory at Woolwich and as their potential ranges increased from about 1000 to 10,000 yards the Royal Navy saw them as having a part to play in the battle line and all British battleships up to 1918 were fitted with underwater tubes capable of firing on the beam. At the very least these were expected to disrupt enemy tactics and perhaps even to cause casualties but they were seldom used at the ranges at which battles were actually fought. Longer ranges were achieved with what were known as 'wet heater' torpedoes. When they were fired, compressed air was released from a chamber inside the torpedo and mixed with atomised fuel to produce a pressurized air/gas mixture at 1000 degrees Centigrade which was fed into the semi-diesel engine cylinders through poppet valves. The combustion chamber was cooled by swirling seawater around its external surface to produce a greater thermal efficiency. The exhaust pipe was central and left a trail of bubbles behind the weapon as it ran, by which it could often be detected. All torpedoes had contra-rotating propellers driven by shafts which revolved around the exhaust pipe; if a single propeller design had been used, the resistance as it tried to turn would have caused the smooth-surfaced torpedo to rotate rather than be propelled forward. Gyros were spun by air from a separate chamber to ensure that the weapon maintained a steady course and depth while running. The four blades visible on the nose of the weapon were impact-sensitive and would detonate the warhead when they were displaced by coming into contact with a target.

COUNTER

Paravanes

A number of devices were considered after 1914 that were thought to be capable of protecting the Grand Fleet against the threat of moored mines. One of these was invented by Commander Usborne, who was serving in the battleship *Colossus,* and he originally described it as a device for 'fending off' any moored mines that might be encountered. His idea was further developed by Lieutenant Burney, son of the Grand Fleet's Second-in-Command, and given the name Paravane. It comprised a short, torpedo-shaped body with fins and a rudder which was streamed from a warship, one on either bow at the end of a wire cable. The first examples were made by the Grand Fleet engineering staff to save time and rushed into service. The fins held the paravane clear of the

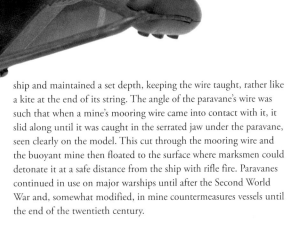

ship and maintained a set depth, keeping the wire taught, rather like a kite at the end of its string. The angle of the paravane's wire was such that when a mine's mooring wire came into contact with it, it slid along until it was caught in the serrated jaw under the paravane, seen clearly on the model. This cut through the mooring wire and the buoyant mine then floated to the surface where marksmen could detonate it at a safe distance from the ship with rifle fire. Paravanes continued in use on major warships until after the Second World War and, somewhat modified, in mine countermeasures vessels until the end of the twentieth century.

Anti-torpedo Nets

The idea of fitting heavy steel-mesh nets which could be suspended from booms along the sides of capital ships dated from about 1876. They hung vertically when the ship was at anchor, descending to the depth of the keel and could be left in place if the ship was moving slowly. 'Out torpedo nets' and 'out boats' booms' were ordered by bugle calls and a ship's efficiency was judged by the speed with which these and other evolutions were carried out during Admirals' Inspections; it was not unknown for them to fall into place unexpectedly after fastenings were loosened to hasten their deployment when ordered! The nets proved to be useless; the old battleship *Majestic* was torpedoed while anchored with her nets out. The *Iron Duke* class was the last class to be built with them and all were removed after 1916. (Photos of *Indomitable* model by Ian Johnston)

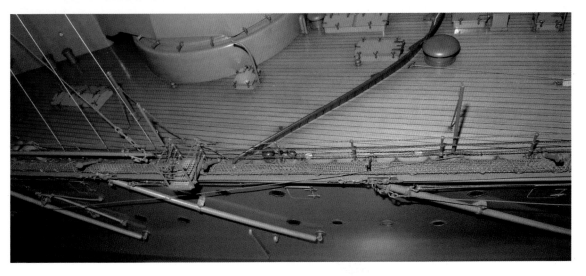

3: Battlecruisers

From the late nineteenth century the Royal Navy built large armoured cruisers with mixed armaments of 9.2-inch, 7.5-inch and 6-inch guns intended to provide heavy support for lighter cruisers on overseas stations and to support battleships in a major fleet action by acting as a fast squadron. *Invincible* and her two sister-ships were initially referred to simply as fast armoured cruisers when they were completed in 1908 but in November 1911 the term 'battlecruiser' was introduced to describe them. Like many of the innovations introduced early in the twentieth century, these ships were the brainchild of Admiral Fisher, who wanted ships that were fast enough to hunt down enemy commerce raiders and destroy them. The introduction of wireless telegraphy and direction-finding technology that could direct a 'flying squadron' of battlecruisers to intercept an enemy force made the concept attractive. Fast enough to hunt down conventional cruisers, they were never intended to fight battleships on their own but were expected to form a fast squadron in the van of the battle fleet to engage enemy ships that were already in action with battleships. Battlecruisers obtained their high speed with machinery of nearly twice the horsepower of contemporary battleships and hulls with significantly less weight devoted to armour. Fisher believed emphatically that speed was the best protection but he seems not to have fully appreciated

the possible result when battlecruisers came into action with other ships of the same type.

The first battlecruiser, *Invincible,* was completed in March 1908 with a deep displacement of 20,135 tons and a main armament of eight 12-inch 45-calibre Mark X guns in twin mountings. A secondary armament of sixteen 4-inch Mark III guns was mounted in casemates and on the turret roofs and intended for use against torpedo boats. The main armoured belt was only 6 inches thick, however, with bulkheads of 6 to 7 inches. Four-shaft machinery of 41,000 horsepower comprising Parsons direct-drive turbines and thirty-one Yarrow coal-burning boilers gave a top speed slightly over 25 knots.

This magnificent 1/48 model of *Indomitable* was made for the Fairfield Shipbuilding & Engineering Company, her builder, and is in the collection of the Museum of Transport in Glasgow. It is outstandingly well detailed and well worth a close study. The anti-torpedo nets are shown rolled up along the deck edge and the wires that held their boom in place can be seen running to cleats on the cable deck. The 4-inch guns on the turret roofs have laying and training hand-wheels and a breech-opening lever. There is even a chart on the table on the upper bridge. Boats, halyards and the standing rigging are all superbly portrayed, as are the wooden decks. A study of this three-dimensional model will give a better 'feel' for this ship than any number of photographs. (Photos by courtesy of Ian Johnston)

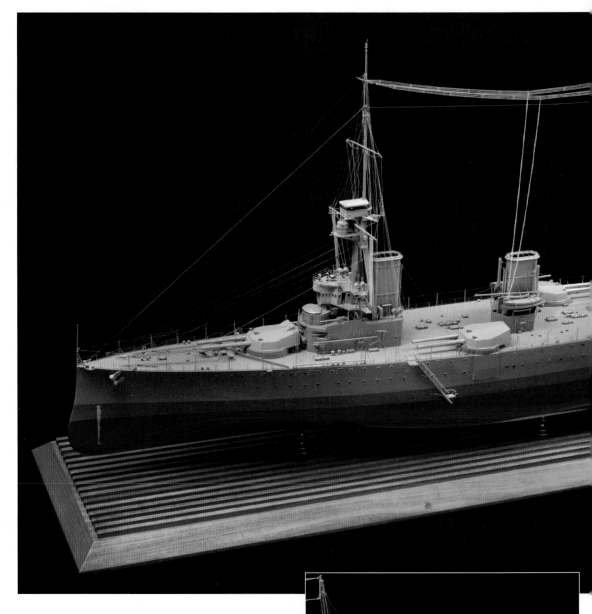

Battlecruiser design evolved through the *Indefatigable* class which comprised, apart from the name-ship, *Australia* built for the Royal Australian Navy and *New Zealand*, which was built for the Royal Navy but paid for by the people of New Zealand since, at the time, there was no separate New Zealand Navy. Tonnage was increased slightly and horsepower increased to 44,000 to give a top speed of over 25 knots.

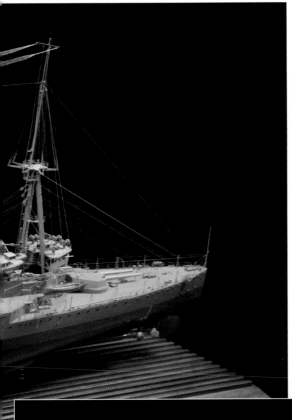

This model of *Australia* was made for the Australian War Memorial by her builder John Brown & Co of Clydebank in the slightly unusual 1/64 scale. It is also unusual in that it was made in 1924 after the ship had been withdrawn from service but largely shows the ship as she appeared when new in 1913. It does, however, have the main armament director below the foretop fitted in 1915 and lacks the anti-torpedo nets which were removed in 1916. It has the original 24-inch searchlight projectors rather than the 36-inch projectors fitted late in the war. The model gives a good idea of the three separated superstructure 'islands' intended to give arcs of fire across the beam for the wing-turrets and the W/T aerials rigged between the masts. The boats with their gold-plated fittings are particularly noticeable. In 1918 aircraft launching platforms were fitted over the roofs and along the barrels of 'P' and 'Q' turrets to allow Sopwith 1½-Strutters to be operated as two-seater, W/T-fitted reconnaissance aircraft. The first such launch took place on 7 March 1918 in the Firth of Forth. (Australian War Memorial)

THE 'SPLENDID CATS'

The *Lion* class of the 1910 Programme represented the next big step. *Lion* and *Princess Royal* had a deep displacement of 29,680 tons and followed contemporary battleship design in mounting 13.5-inch 45-calibre guns (four twin turrets) with sixteen 4-inch guns as an anti-torpedo-boat defence. Four-shaft machinery with Parsons turbines and no less than forty-two coal-fired boilers augmented by fuel oil sprayers developed 70,000 horsepower. Designed speed was 27 knots, which could be exceeded with good quality coal supplied constantly to skilled stokers working the furnaces. At the time of her completion in Devonport Dockyard in 1912, *Lion* was the largest and fastest capital ship ever built.

This scratch-built 1/128 model of *Lion* by the well-known professional modelmaker John R Haynes shows her as she appeared in 1918 with flying-off platforms on 'Q' and 'Y' turrets, the latter built so that the aircraft took off over the after end of the turret to lessen the angle it needed to turn to point the aircraft into the 'felt' wind, which was usually ahead of the beam. Despite its relatively small size, the detailing on this model is very good and the Sopwith 2F.1 Camel fighters on the launching platforms, boats, bridge details and rigging are particularly well constructed. By 1918 the majority of the Grand Fleet's battleships and battlecruisers carried one or two aircraft with over 100 embarked when the whole fleet was at sea. Note the bearing indicators painted onto 'Y' turret and the distinctive clinker screen added to the forward funnel. She was Admiral Beatty's flagship at Jutland when a shell penetrated the junction of the face and roof of 'Q' turret, blowing half of it away and igniting cordite which could have destroyed her had the officer of the turret, Major Harvey RM, who was mortally wounded, not given the order to flood the magazine. *Lion* was eventually withdrawn from service in 1923, only ten years old, and scrapped at Jarrow under the terms of the Washington Naval Treaty. (By courtesy of John R Haynes)

A third, slightly modified, ship of the *Lion* class was completed a year later than the first two and named *Queen Mary*. With the later *Tiger*, they were known as the 'Splendid Cats'.

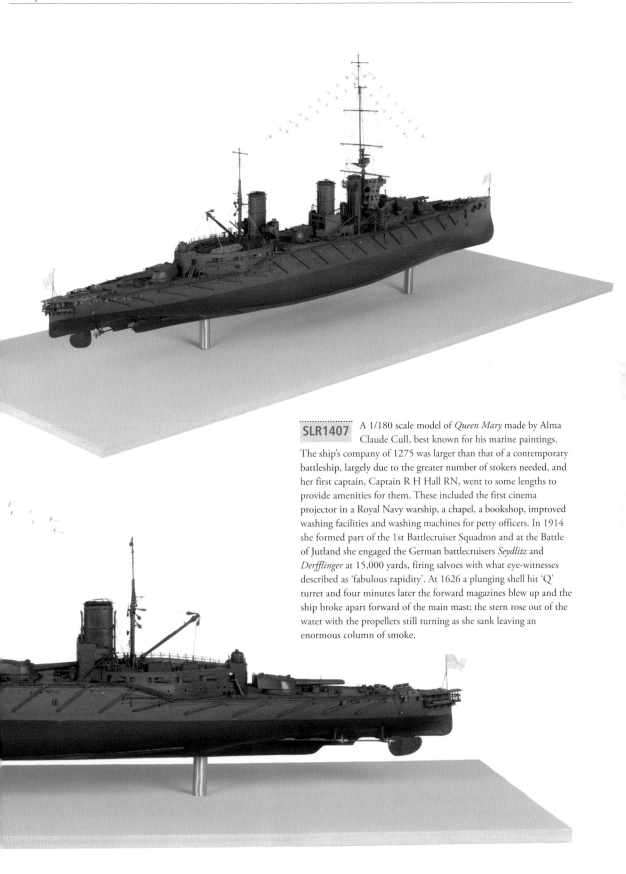

SLR1407 A 1/180 scale model of *Queen Mary* made by Alma Claude Cull, best known for his marine paintings. The ship's company of 1275 was larger than that of a contemporary battleship, largely due to the greater number of stokers needed, and her first captain, Captain R H Hall RN, went to some lengths to provide amenities for them. These included the first cinema projector in a Royal Navy warship, a chapel, a bookshop, improved washing facilities and washing machines for petty officers. In 1914 she formed part of the 1st Battlecruiser Squadron and at the Battle of Jutland she engaged the German battlecruisers *Seydlitz* and *Derfflinger* at 15,000 yards, firing salvoes with what eye-witnesses described as 'fabulous rapidity'. At 1626 a plunging shell hit 'Q' turret and four minutes later the forward magazines blew up and the ship broke apart forward of the main mast; the stern rose out of the water with the propellers still turning as she sank leaving an enormous column of smoke.

FEATURES OF A CAPITAL SHIP

This builder's model shows *Queen Mary* in 1913, lacking the modifications later fitted to capital ships in the light of war experience. These included paravanes, large searchlights for night fighting, platforms for launching aircraft, a new primary director on an enlarged spotting top and a larger, more enclosed bridge structure. Capital ships were the most technologically advanced weapons systems ever devised before 1914. Their offensive power lay in their big guns, in *Queen Mary*'s case eight 13.5-inch Mark V guns in four twin Mark II* turrets. Pre-war concepts that guns might have to operate in local control at short range after damage to primary systems led to the fitting, in each turret, of sighting hoods for the layer, trainer and turret officer. However, war experience showed these could detonate shells that would, otherwise, have glanced off a smooth, sloping turret roof and cause serious explosions and fire which could rapidly find its way to the magazines through the ammunition supply routes.

Queen Mary had forty-two boilers working at 235psi to provide steam for Parsons geared turbines on four shafts, developing 70,000 horsepower (more than double that of a contemporary battleship) to give a maximum

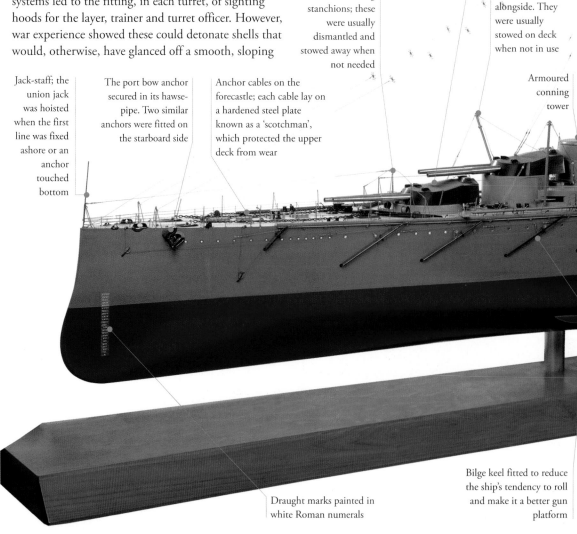

'A' turret with its twin 13.5-inch guns; the sighting ports show prominently on the sloping roof. The other turrets, from forward 'B', 'Q' and 'Y', were identical

Derricks in their operating position; used to hoist coal, ammunition and stores inboard from lighters alongside. They were usually stowed on deck when not in use

Awning stanchions; these were usually dismantled and stowed away when not needed

Jack-staff; the union jack was hoisted when the first line was fixed ashore or an anchor touched bottom

The port bow anchor secured in its hawse-pipe. Two similar anchors were fitted on the starboard side

Anchor cables on the forecastle; each cable lay on a hardened steel plate known as a 'scotchman', which protected the upper deck from wear

Armoured conning tower

Bilge keel fitted to reduce the ship's tendency to roll and make it a better gun platform

Draught marks painted in white Roman numerals

speed of about 27 knots. This was 6 knots faster than a battleship of the *King George V* class, although the actual speed achieved depended on the number and skill of the stokers and the quality of the coal in use.

Dreadnought and her immediate successors had officers' accommodation amidships, under the bridge, but *Queen Mary* reverted to a more traditional arrangement with officers aft and an admiral's stern walk right aft. The pole fore mast carried a small spotting top over the bridge and yardarms from which groups of signal flags were hoisted. The bridge structure

just forward of it was basic with an exposed compass platform. The box-like structure beneath it contains sea cabins for the admiral, captain and navigating officer and forward of it is the armoured conning tower with its narrow, slit openings from which the ship could be controlled in action, although, in practice, the majority of captains chose to fight their ships from the compass platform where they had greater situational awareness and control. Wireless telegraphy aerials feature prominently, rigged from the highest point of the fore mast.

Spotting top from which the main armament's fall of shot was observed and corrections ordered to guns

Fore mast with yardarms for flag signal hoists

Wireless telegraphy aerials rigged from the highest point of the mast to give the maximum range possible

Bridge structure surmounted by the compass platform. Painted canvas screens known as 'dodgers' were fitted over the guardrails to give some protection against the wind

Main mast with a derrick for lowering boats. The larger pinnaces were powered by steam and could carry small guns and lightweight torpedoes for inshore operations. Sea-boats were carried on davits from which they could be lowered quickly into the water

After rangefinder for the main armament

Admiral's stern gallery, accessed through his harbour day cabin

Rudder

Two port shafts; the propellers were made of phosphor-bronze

Secondary armament of sixteen 4-inch 50-calibre guns mounted four on each quarter in casemates to give all-round coverage against attacking torpedo boats at close range

Port after ladder in the lowered position; used by officers to access boats

Rolled anti-torpedo nets in their stowed position along the deck edge. Their use was discontinued from 1916 and they were removed

One of the eighteen booms that supported the nets on each side of the ship in their stowed position; they lay out horizontally in use, keeping the nets away from the ship's side

SLR1408

CAPITAL SHIP DEVELOPMENT 1914-1918

ENLARGED BRIDGE-WORK

SLR1401 *Conqueror's* small bridge is typical of structures before 1914 with a compass binnacle on the exposed compass platform over the small charthouse. Some protection for those on the bridge would have been provided by a painted canvas 'dodger' fitted to the guardrails, not shown on the model. The armoured conning tower, from which the ship was supposed to be controlled in action, can be seen forward of the bridge with the narrow slit through which officers would have had their only view of the action. It has a small main armament director on top of it. The small. open spotting top was frequently rendered uninhabitable by funnel gases having been badly sited aft of the fore funnel.

SLR1403 By 1918 *Iron Duke* showed significant progress in the development of bridge and gunnery control arrangements. The compass platform is still basic but the box-like structure beneath it provides space for a chart-room and sea cabins for the admiral, captain and navigating officer. A larger director with its own rangefinder is mounted on the conning tower and the spotting top has been enlarged and enclosed with a main armament director fitted on top. 'B' turret has been painted with deflection scales and there is a range-indicating 'clock' on the spotting top. These, and similar measures aft, allowed ships in company to train and aim their own guns for group firing even if they could not, themselves, initially see the target.

SLR1414 *Queen Elizabeth's* bridge structure is seen here after her 1925-27 reconstruction, showing the full extent of RN wartime experience. The enlarged spotting top is fully enclosed with a main armament director on top fitted with its own rangefinder. The compass platform is better screened and partially enclosed against the elements with an enlarged structure under it housing a tactical plot, staff offices, sea cabins and a less cramped charthouse. Rangefinders are fitted above the compass platform, in the lower director and in each turret.

SEARCHLIGHTS

As completed, the battlecruiser *Australia* shows an array of 24-inch searchlights mounted in pairs on the after superstructure. They were only effective at short range and their operators – officially known as 'manipulators' – were completely exposed in action, with no target indication from the bridge. They were intended, principally, for use with the secondary armament against attack by torpedo boats. In 1914 the Grand Fleet regarded night action as leaving too much to chance; it was not well equipped or trained for it and sought to avoid it whenever possible. (Australian War Memorial)

SLR1401 *Conqueror*'s after superstructure shows an evolutionary stage of night-fighting capability with paired 24-inch searchlights mounted around the secondary compass platform aft. Mounted close together they were easier to co-ordinate but still lacked the range to be effective enough for the main armament.

Lion shows the wartime improvements that made the Grand Fleet into an effective night-fighting force by 1918. Large 36-inch searchlights can be seen fitted in clusters around the after funnel; they are fitted on top of splinter-proof towers occupied by the manipulators. Targets were allocated to them from the bridge by Evershed indicators and they could view them through slits to keep the searchlights on target. Night fighting was no longer regarded as a matter of chance in 1918 when the Grand Fleet had become equally proficient by night and day. (By courtesy of John R Haynes)

SECONDARY ARMAMENT

Indomitable, like the other battlecruisers of the *Invincible* class, mounted a secondary armament of sixteen 4-inch 45-calibre quick-firing guns with two on each turret roof to give all-round fire against torpedo boats attacking at close range. This arrangement was not a success because the guns' crews were completely exposed and blast prevented them from standing-to when the main armament was in action. Blast from the big guns also caused shock damage to the mountings. (By courtesy of Ian Johnston)

SLR1407 *Queen Mary* shows the next evolutionary step with sixteen 4-inch 50-calibre quick-firing guns, mounted in the two superstructure blocks with four on each quarter to give all-round fire. The guns are fitted in casemates, which gave their crews protection against splinters and the weather, besides allowing them to remain stood-to when the main armament was in action.

SLR1401 *Queen Elizabeth* shows the secondary armament of 6-inch 45-calibre guns, considered better able than the earlier 4-inch to deal with the larger destroyers then coming into service; but the slower rate of fire of the larger gun was a concern. Fitted in casemates along the hull, four of the original sixteen were positioned even lower under the quarterdeck; these constantly flooded in even a moderate sea and were soon removed.

AIRCRAFT AND AA

By 1918 the majority of battleships and battlecruisers in the Grand
Fleet had been modified with turret platforms to operate aircraft;
over 100 were routinely embarked by the end of the war. *Lion* was
fitted with a platform on 'Q' turret and a Sopwith 2.F1 'Ship' Camel
can be seen on it. The turret was turned into the relative wind to
launch the aircraft so that the ship itself did not have to alter course.
With no means of recovering the aircraft, it had to ditch after its
sortie and *Lion* is known to have launched at least five different
Camels. A Sopwith 1½-Strutter spotter/reconnaissance aircraft was
carried on a larger platform on 'Y' turret. Of interest, note the
4-inch high-angle anti-aircraft mounted on the upper
deck reflecting the need to defend against enemy
aircraft when the Camel was not available.
(By courtesy of John R Haynes)

H M S HOOD

The ultimate expression of British battlecruiser design was *Hood* which was laid down in 1916 but after Jutland the design was modified to include more armour. She remained capable of 31 knots, however, and at 860 feet overall, she was the longest warship ever to serve with the Royal Navy in the twentieth century. Completed in 1920, she cost £6,025,000 and required machinery of 144,000 shaft horsepower to achieve her high speed.

SLR1403 This 1/600 waterline model by Roger Chesneau shows *Hood* as she appeared in the Second World War steaming at high speed. Twin 4-inch high-angle mountings have replaced the original low-angle 5.5-inch guns as secondary armament and the unsuccessful unrotated projectile launchers are mounted on the roof of 'B' turret. In May 1941 *Hood* was lost in action with *Bismarck* when enemy shells penetrated an after magazine, leading to a series of explosions that caused the ship to disintegrate; there were only 3 survivors out of a ship's company of 1477.

4: Cruisers

Cruisers evolved from the frigates of the nineteenth century and were broadly defined as ships capable of independent operations on distant stations, able to fight any opponent other than a capital ship, and adaptable to a wide variety of tasks. They had the fuel stowage and workshops to enable them to undertake long periods without support from depot ships or bases. After 1890 cruisers were reclassified according to a system in which First Class ships had 9.2-inch guns and were capable of acting as a fast squadron of the battle fleet, although not of engaging battleships independently. Second Class ships had 6-inch guns; Third Class ships had lesser guns and were not expected to work with the fleet. They were spread throughout the British Empire to protect trade and British interests. All sailors were given military training and, as well as landing Royal Marines, cruisers were expected to be able to land a company of 'bluejackets', usually stokers, for operations on land when required. Some of the lighter ship's guns were designed to be dismounted and fitted on wheeled carriages for operations ashore, the origin of the Field Gun Competition which is still familiar in military tournaments. The ability of cruisers to spread their influence from the sea onto the land in this manner

may have given the First Lord of the Admiralty, Winston Churchill, the germ of the idea to form a Royal Naval Division for operations on land in 1914.

By 1905 the large, protected cruisers of the old first class were reduced to reserve, their role being taken over in the next decade by battlecruisers. Ships that survived after 1914 were used for subsidiary duties, dispersed to remote stations where they were unlikely to see action, or expended as block-ships. Admiral

Fisher had originally no intention of including cruisers in his modernised fleet but experience showed that battlecruisers on their own were too expensive to provide a large fleet with all the reconnaissance it needed and, at the other end of the spectrum, as a cruiser-substitute the large destroyer *Swift* proved to be a disappointment in service. In response, a series of fast, light cruisers were built, starting with the *Bristol* class of five ships completed in 1910. In 1911 the old system of classification was discontinued, the larger armoured ships becoming known simply as cruisers, and the new ships, all of which were named after cities

and towns, as light cruisers. Steady evolution of the design brought a series of classes after *Bristol*, including the *Weymouth*, *Chatham* and *Birmingham* classes. Three ships of the *Chatham* class were built for the Royal Australian Navy, two of which, *Melbourne* and *Sydney*, served with the Grand Fleet. By 1918 town names were replaced by classes of ships with names which began with the same letter of the alphabet; first the 'C's and then the 'D's and further construction evolved through the *Caroline*, *Cambrian* and *Centaur* classes. Light cruisers bore the brunt of fighting in the North Sea, and many continued in service after 1919.

SLR0039 *Gibraltar* was laid down in 1889 and this highly detailed 1/48 scale model was made by her builder, William Beardmore of Dalmuir on the Clyde. She was one of nine First Class protected cruisers of the *Edgar* class; well-liked ships with an armament of two 9.2-inch and ten 6-inch guns. She had triple-expansion steam engines driving two shafts and four double-ended, coal-fired boilers. Top speed was 19 knots and the whole class had a reputation for being mechanically reliable in service. One of *Gibraltar*'s sister-ships steamed at 18 knots – effectively full speed – for 48 hours. She had four submerged 18-inch torpedo tubes with a number of reloads and a 5-inch armoured deck.

Like all builder's models, this one shows considerable detail. The single 9.2-inch guns are visible fore and aft with the 6-inch guns distributed around the central superstructure. Boats are stowed inboard and on davits with derricks rigged to work the former; all fittings are gold- and silver-plated so that they stand out against their backgrounds. The large number of ventilators visible around the funnels were there to draw air into the boilers. The hull below the real ship's waterline was sheathed in copper as an antifouling measure and this is accurately represented on the model.

Like her sister-ships, *Gibraltar* spent her early life deployed outside the UK, in the Mediterranean, South Atlantic and the America and West Indies Stations between 1894 and 1906. Reduced to a nucleus ship's company in Devonport, she was brought forward to escort the new destroyers *Parramatta* and *Yarra* to Australia in 1910/11. By 1914 she was in use as a depot ship for the anti-submarine school at Portland but on the outbreak of war she joined the 10th Cruiser Squadron which formed the Northern Patrol, guarding the northern entrances to the North Sea to prevent German shipping from evading the British blockade. When armed merchant cruisers more suited to the task became available in 1915, she was disarmed and used as a depot ship for the Northern Patrol, based in the Shetland Islands until 1918. In 1919 she returned to the anti-submarine school as a depot ship until 1922 when she was withdrawn from service and scrapped.

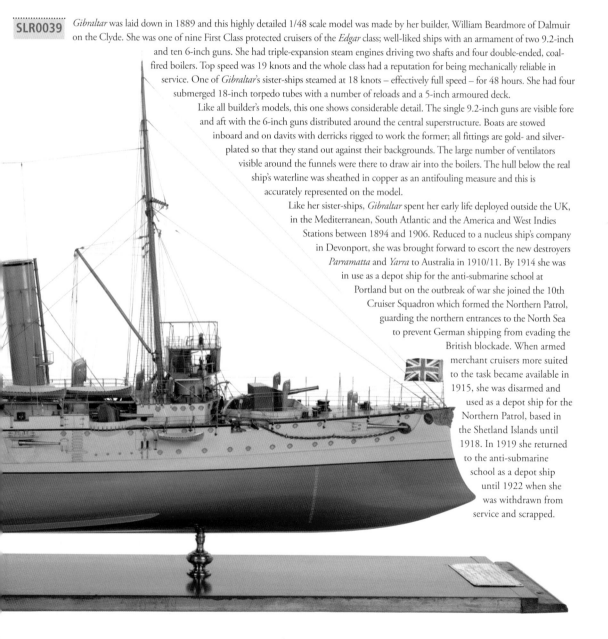

ARMOURED CRUISERS

Earlier RN cruisers had relied on a protective armoured deck for defence against shellfire (and hence were usually classified as 'protected cruisers'), but the advent of face-hardened steel armour in the mid-1890s allowed a comparatively large area of the hull sides to be armoured as well; the new ships with this form of protection were known as armoured cruisers. The first of these were the six 12,000-ton *Cressy* class ordered in 1898.

By the outbreak of war in August 1914 they were obsolescent, but five of class formed the 7th Cruiser Squadron. The following month three of them, the *Cressy, Aboukir* and *Hogue*, were being used to patrol an area of the southern North Sea known as the 'Broad Fourteens' off the Dutch coast. They were intended to provide distant cover for the movement of troops to France but were themselves exposed by the lack of immediate cover by capital ships, and rough weather in

the previous days had prevented them from having any destroyer escort. By dawn on 22 September the weather had abated and the ships were cruising slowly in company without taking any evasive measures. At 0630 *Aboukir* was hit by a torpedo from *U 9* and began to sink. Thinking that she had struck a mine, *Hogue* closed her to pick up survivors and was, in turn, torpedoed by *U 9*. Seeing both her sister-ships sinking, *Cressy* stopped among the survivors. By then *U 9* had surfaced and *Cressy* opened fire on her before she, too, was torpedoed and sunk. Between them, the three cruisers lost 1449 men; among them were many from an entire term of Dartmouth cadets that had been embarked to gain sea experience. This incident taught the Royal Navy hard lessons about the new technology and tactics required in naval warfare.

This finely-detailed waterline model from the Imperial War Museum's collection depicts *Cressy,* the name ship of a class of six armoured cruisers. She was built by Fairfield at Govan and completed in 1901. The design was based on the earlier *Diadem* class protected cruisers, but with two single 9.2-inch guns replacing four of the earlier ship's sixteen 6-inch guns. Her forward and after secondary 6-inch guns were mounted in the same unsatisfactory double-tiered casemates, with the lower guns difficult, if not impossible, to use in rough seas. The guns mounted between them, although not double-tiered were also too close to the waterline. This 1/192 scale model was made by Julian Glossop and shows the ship as she appeared in 1914. Rigging and boats are well formed with larger boats stowed on deck aft of the after funnel below the derrick used to launch them. Two boats are suspended from davits and the forward one is a sea-boat with white painted gripes holding it firmly in place. The forward boat boom can be seen in its stowed position just aft of the forward, lower 6-inch casemate. (Imperial War Museum MOD000603)

The *Drake* class was a logical development of the earlier *Cressy* class armoured cruisers with improved machinery making them among the world's fastest major warships at the time of their completion (some exceeded their design speed of 23 knots on trials). Referred to by Lord Goschen, the First Lord of the Admiralty, as 'mighty cruisers', they were also unusual for their time in being able to steam for long distances at high speed. In terms of armament they showed less progress, however, with their secondary 6-inch guns mounted one above the other in four double casemates on each side of the hull. The lower guns were close to the waterline and proved to be impossible to work in rough weather. They had an armoured belt along the side of the hull which was 6 inches at its thickest point, tapering to 3 inches at either end with a full armoured deck 3 inches thick at the centre, tapering to 1 inch at the bow and stern. As a type, however, they were soon rendered obsolescent by battlecruisers.

SLR1326 *Leviathan* was one of the four ships of the *Drake* class that formed part of the 1898 Construction Programme and this 1/48 model was made by her builder, John Brown of Clydebank. It is exceptionally well detailed and many of its finer points are beautiful little models in their own right. It shows her as she appeared when completed in 1903, shortly before the Royal Navy adopted a grey paint scheme for ships on the Home Station.

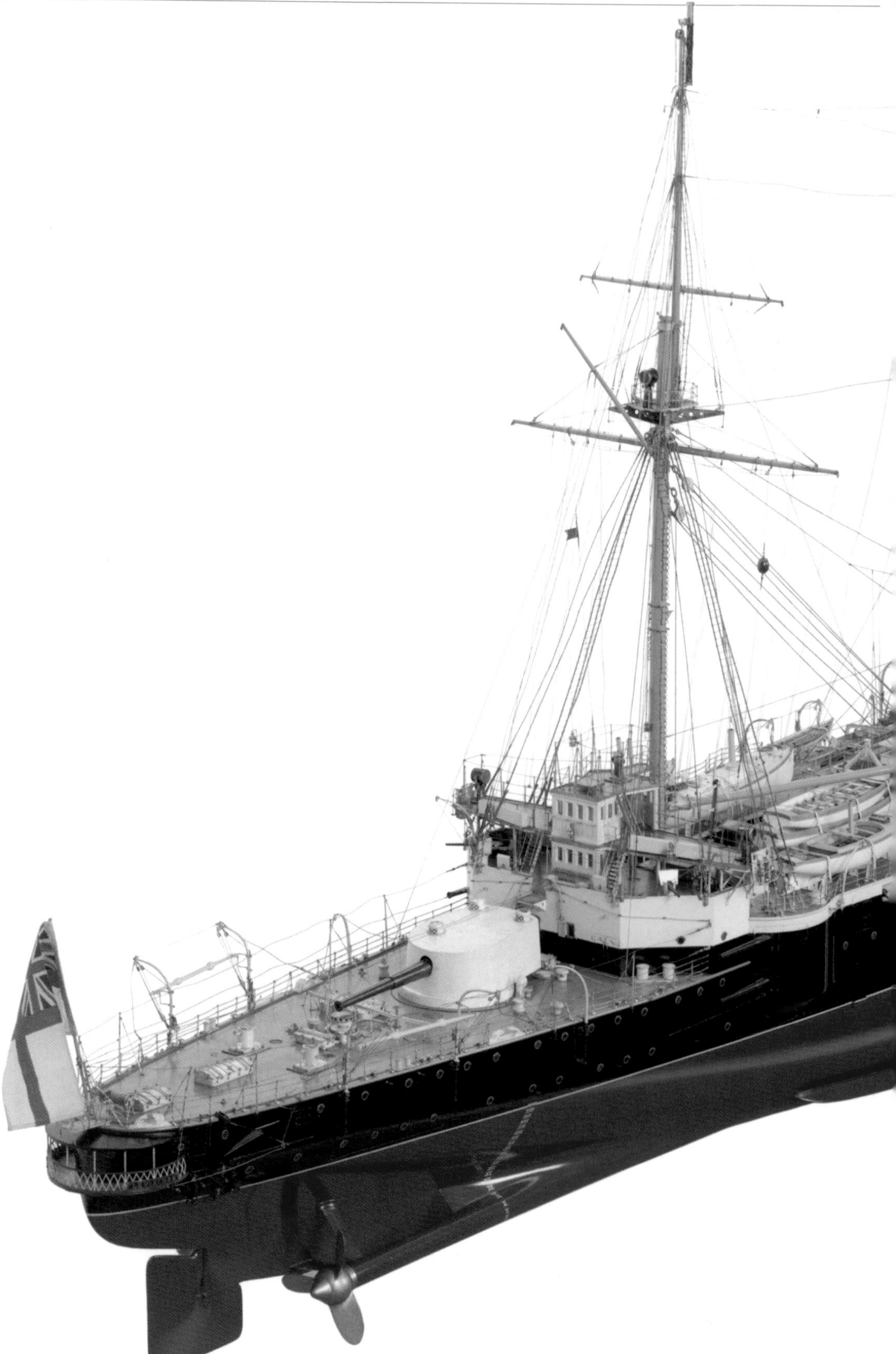

SLR1326 *Leviathan*: the lower 6-inch guns in their double casements stand out clearly, as does the fully-detailed rigging. Anchors, cables, boats and the bridge are all finely detailed. The bridge wings were intended both to give the captain a good view over the side when coming alongside in harbour and space for signalmen to work at flag-hoists, semaphore and the use of the signal lamps at the outer edge while at sea. The enclosed bridge contains a ship's wheel and compass binnacle, features that are replicated in the secondary conning position aft of the main mast. The three after funnels are lozenge-shaped and the forward one is circular, indicating the differing number of boilers connected to it. Seventeen boats are stowed on deck or suspended from davits; three of the boats stowed aft of the funnels are steam pinnaces, each capable of being armed with quick-firing guns and torpedoes in their own right to attack enemy vessels in harbour. Mechanical semaphore arms are located in the bridge wing and at the top of the main mast; other details include hose reels, winches and a number of small guns. The whole class, including *Leviathan*, were intended to be used as cruiser squadron flagships on distant stations and they all had a stern walk right aft, opening out of the admiral's harbour accommodation.

Leviathan was laid down in 1899 and completed on 3 July 1901. She spent her early years on the Home, Channel, Mediterranean and America and West Indies Stations before becoming the flagship of the Training Squadron in UK waters during 1912. In 1913 she was reduced to a lower degree of readiness and formed part of the 6th Cruiser Squadron in the Third, or Reserve, Fleet. In 1914 she was brought out of reserve with other ships of the 6th, but in December she transferred to the 5th Cruiser squadron which formed part of the Grand Fleet. Her gunnery systems were no longer up to the standard required by the principal fleet, however, and in 1915 she became the flagship of the America and West Indies Station where she looked impressive without too much risk of having to fight a superior opponent. In 1918 she joined other ships in escorting Atlantic convoys and in 1919 she was replaced as the flagship on station and returned to the UK where she was paid off and sold for scrap in 1920.

SLR1326 *Leviathan*'s amidships area showing the wealth of deck detail in this model, especially the boats. Note the stepping rungs on the side of the hull between the casemates to give access from boats alongside; they are very similar to those in *Victory* built over a century earlier. A number of quick-firing 3-pounders and Maxim machine-guns are fitted on the upper deck to give a 'last ditch' defence against small torpedo-craft at close range.

SLR1326 The secondary or after bridge, with 3-pounders and Maxim machine-guns mounted behind the screen ahead of the after 9.2-inch turret, which has sighting hoods for the layer, trainer and turret captain. The after bridge duplicated much of the equipment on the main bridge, including the semaphore arm and signal lanterns on the bridge wings, the compass platform with its binnacle over the secondary steering position; there is an engine telegraph and revolution telegraph by the wheelhouse. The wheels for the ship's landing guns are stowed under the bridge wings.

SLR1326 Midship detail showing steam pinnaces stowed to port and cutters to starboard. A whaler is turned inboard on davits and rope falls are stowed realistically on drums, ready for use. Note the derrick attached to the main mast which was used to lower boats into the water and recover them. It was hand operated with seamen pulling on ropes. The white hatches amidships were opened at sea to provide light and ventilation to the engine rooms below. Note also the after, or secondary, compass platform and wheelhouse with wings similar to the primary position forward. The cruciform shape stowed on the wing extremity is a 'fog-buoy' towed astern to create a splash at a safe distance on which other ships could keep station in fog.

SLR1326 Detail of *Leviathan*'s main top showing the small aft-facing signal lantern.

SLR1326 Bow detail showing the ram which was thought to be of value as a weapon in the late nineteenth century but of little value at the ranges ships fought at in the First World War. Note the 'bow-chaser' 12-pounder guns in their embrasures and the way anchors were stowed before the introduction of stockless anchors in the early twentieth century. Two anchors were fitted on this side (only one to port) and the blanked off apertures led down to the cable locker. If left open at sea, they could allow water to flood the cable locker, which was one good reason for the subsequent adoption of cable led up onto the forecastle from below leading across hardened plates known as 'scotchmen' to stockless anchors in hawsepipes.

SLR1326 *Leviathan*'s compass platform and wheelhouse seen from the port side. Note the Maxim machine-gun and semaphore arm near the signal lantern and the superbly detailed deck fittings. Note the circular, armoured conning tower below the wheelhouse from which the ship could be fought in action.

SLR1326 The fore funnel showing its bracing wires and the brass sirens with their steam supply pipes fitted to the small platform half way up. The boats suspended from davits, drums of rope and lockers on the upper deck are all beautiful models in their own right.

CRUISER DESIGNS FOR EXPORT

Britain dominated the world market for iron-hulled warships with steam propulsion from 1860 with as much as half the design effort of major firms being devoted to battleships, cruisers and destroyers for the export market. Armstrong on the Tyne, for instance, had an international reputation for their cruiser designs and were proud of having built a number of the Japanese ships that defeated the Russian fleet at the Battle of Tsushima. Vickers built ships for both the Russian and Japanese fleets. These exported ships benefited the British economy, allowed firms to experiment with novel designs that were not necessarily aimed at RN requirements and supported the world's largest shipbuilding infrastructure within the UK, which could be turned to national advantage in wartime. Besides completed ships, Britain also exported naval architectural expertise: for example, these models were among six presented to the Royal Naval College at Greenwich in 1910 as a token of gratitude for the consideration shown to the Japanese constructors, engineers and naval officers who had studied there.

SLR1334 This 1/48 builder's model of the Japanese cruiser *Niitaka* was made by Yokosuka Navy Yard and shows the ship as she appeared on her completion in 1902. Although she was built in Japan, her design shows significant British influence and resembles the RN *Sirius* class protected cruisers. Coal-fired boilers and triple-expansion steam engines gave her a speed of 20 knots and she was well thought of in service. She took part in the Japanese attack on the Russian fleet in Port Arthur and in the Battle of Tsushima in 1905 and remained in service until accidentally wrecked in 1922. It is of a quality comparable with the best British builders' models and shows their influence by being made to the same scale. It was intended to be impressive and even the smallest details are beautifully made and plated in gold or silver to stand out. The bridge is a masterpiece, complete with a shutter telegraph, awning frame, chart table, binnacle and sash windows. The prominent ram bow is clearly evident.

SLR1384 Another of the models presented to the Royal Naval College Greenwich by the Imperial Japanese Navy in 1910, this 1/48 scale builder's model depicts *Mogami*, which was originally described as a small protected cruiser but subsequently listed as a dispatch vessel. She was built at Nagasaki and lightly armed with two 4.7-inch and two 3-inch guns. She was 311 feet long and had a speed of 23 knots, which was already modest for a cruiser when she was completed in 1908. She was finally withdrawn from service in 1928. The model's dark grey hull and funnels make the wooden-planked deck and the gold- and silver-plated fittings stand out; the fine anchor cable, guardrails, ladders and bridge instruments are particularly noteworthy. The two torpedo tubes on the upper deck have been gun-metalled to make them look realistic and the rigging is authentically reproduced with the gaff at the top of the pole mast used to attach wireless telegraphy aerials.

SCOUT CRUISERS

After 1900, as torpedo boat destroyers developed realistic sea-keeping qualities that enabled them to operate in the open ocean, a new type of cruiser evolved that was intended to locate and shadow the enemy fleet, command and control destroyer flotillas, lead torpedo attacks and back up destroyers with gunfire when they were required to repel an attack by the enemy's flotillas. Four classes, each of two ships, were built in quick succession from 1904 onwards, comprising vessels that proved to be an evolutionary step between the earlier Third Class cruisers and the subsequent generation of light cruisers. They were known, initially, as scout cruisers. All eight ships were built to broad Admiralty specifications by firms with experience of destroyer construction, but there were significant differences between them.

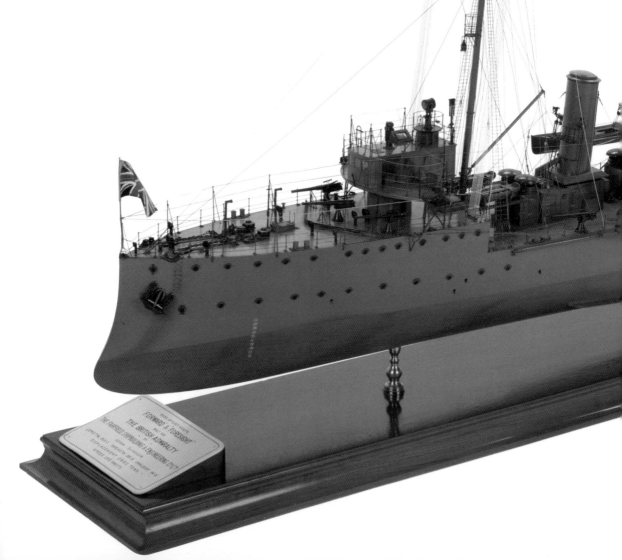

SLR0015 *Forward* was built by Fairfield at Govan, laid down on 22 October 1903 and completed in August 1905, and this 1/48 scale full hull model was made by her builder to show the ship in accurate detail as she appeared when she left the yard. She was 379 feet long with a displacement of 2860 tons and she was powered by two-shaft, three-cylinder triple-expansion steam engines with twelve Thornycroft boilers delivering 16,500 horsepower, which gave her a top speed of 25 knots. The boilers were coal-fired and her bunkers had capacity for 500 tons, giving only a limited radius of action, but at the time the destroyers she was intended to lead were not expected to operate far from their bases. She was lightly armoured with a half-inch deck and 2-inch belt abreast the machinery and her armament reflected the requirement to bring a great deal of rapid fire to bear on the enemy in a high-speed, close-quarter melee. For this reason she was initially armed with ten 12-pounder, unshielded, quick-firing guns. She was not intended to fight enemy cruisers but the two 18-inch torpedo tubes on the upper deck aft of the after funnel gave her the ability to engage larger warships or take part in her flotilla's attacks. The three forward guns are fitted ahead of the bridge, three are on the raised poop, and the

others are mounted along the sides of the deck further aft. Boats are rigged to davits and the open bridge has a covered chart table and other navigational equipment. The single pole mast has a high gaff fitted to it from which wireless telegraphy aerials were rigged.

Forward spent her first two years after completion with a nucleus ship's company in reserve at Portsmouth before becoming leader of the 2nd Destroyer Flotilla in the Home Fleet in 1909. In 1910 she was attached to the 4th Destroyer Flotilla at Portsmouth and re-armed with nine 4-inch guns, bringing her into line with the new light cruisers. She was also fitted with a single 3-inch anti-aircraft gun. Later in 1910 she joined the 3rd Destroyer Flotilla at the Nore until the outbreak of war when she joined the 9th Destroyer Flotilla which formed the Shetland Island Patrol. During 1915 she served in the Humber but was considered too slow for work with light cruisers or destroyers on operations in the North Sea and she moved to the Mediterranean Fleet where she remained on escort duties until 1918 when she returned to the Nore to pay off. She was sold for scrap in 1921.

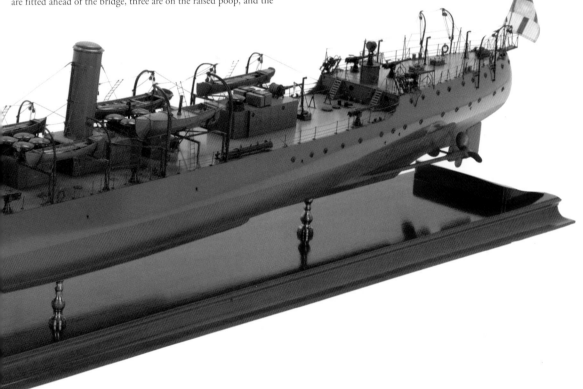

LIGHT CRUISERS

By 1909 the older, small cruisers and the newer scout cruisers had evolved into the light cruiser, one of the most prominent warship types used in the First World War. This was a return to traditional cruiser requirements, in between the extremes of armoured cruisers (in effect second class battleships) and the 'scouts', which were little more than destroyer leaders. Designed to combine speed, protection, firepower and sea-keeping, the new cruisers were built in four incrementally improved groups, all named after towns. The third group was the *Chatham* class, three ships of

which were built for the Royal Navy and a further three for the Royal Australian Navy. One of the latter was HMAS *Sydney*, superbly represented by this model in the Australian National Maritime Museum.

At 1/100 scale, the model is finely detailed and accurately depicts *Sydney* as she appeared in service. Displacing 6000 tons deep load, she was armed with eight 6-inch guns in open shields and two submerged 21-inch torpedo tubes on the beam. The guns were disposed with one on the centreline on the forecastle, one on either side of the bridge; one on either side of the third funnel; one on either side at the break of the quarterdeck and one on the

centreline of the quarterdeck further aft. With this arrangement only five guns could be fired on either beam and only three directly ahead or astern. She has been fitted with a spotting top on the tripod fore mast, on the roof of which is a director that controlled the fire of all the guns. She has not yet been fitted with the rotatable aircraft-launching platform added forward of the bridge in 1918, however. The absence of scuttles low on the port side amidships shows where the 2-inch armour belt was fitted to the ship's side and she had a full armoured deck which was 1.5 inches thick over the machinery, tapering to 0.5 of an inch forward and aft. *Sydney* had four-shaft machinery with Parsons turbines and twelve Yarrow boilers developing 25,000 shaft horsepower, giving her a speed of slightly over 25 knots. The deck is covered with realistic looking wood planking.

Sydney was built by the London and Glasgow Shipbuilding Company at Govan and completed in June 1913. Together with the battlecruiser *Australia* and her sister-ship *Melbourne*, she formed part of the first entry of the Royal Australian Navy fleet unit into Sydney harbour in October 1913. She served in the Pacific in 1914, sinking the German cruiser *Emden* in a famous 'ship-versus-ship' action on 9 November 1914. She subsequently joined the America and West Indies Station until 1916 when she joined the 2nd Light Cruiser squadron in the Grand Fleet. In 1919 she returned to Australia and continued in service until May 1928. She was broken up in Cockatoo Island Dockyard in 1929-30 but her tripod fore mast was removed and mounted on Bradley's head in Sydney Harbour where it still stands in 2014 as a memorial. (Australian National Maritime Museum)

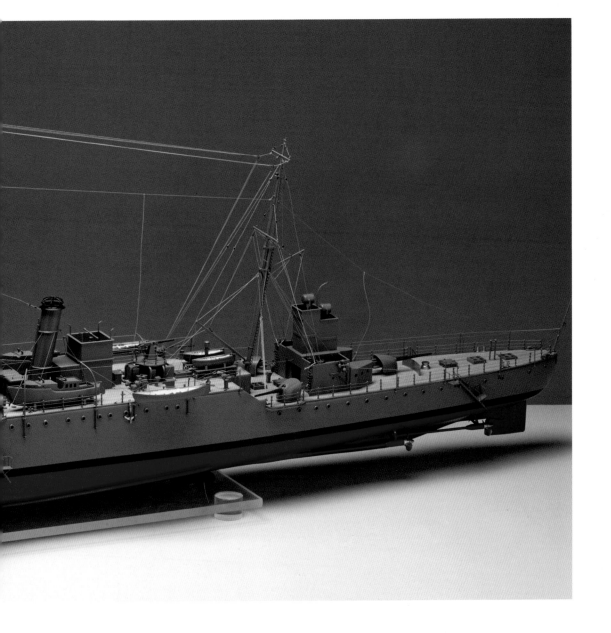

FEATURES OF A LIGHT CRUISER

The only vessel left afloat that fought at Jutland, and the most important British warship of that era, is the cruiser *Caroline*, currently at Belfast in the care of the National Museum of the Royal Navy. Fortunately the National Maritime Museum's collection contains this fine 1/48 scale builder's model of *Caroline*,

Single 6-inch guns in open shields. The concept behind this arrangement was that in advancing to locate the enemy battle fleet or to oppose an enemy torpedo attack she would come into close-quarter conflict with destroyers at high speed and would need 4-inch quick-firing guns in some numbers to engage fleeting targets over open sights. If forced to withdraw by a superior enemy she would need deliberate fire from heavier guns capable of greater hitting power, hence the 6-inch guns aft.

After, secondary, rangefinder position also used as a secondary compass platform

Starboard twin 21-inch torpedo tubes on a rotatable mounting. They were aimed from the compass platform

Single unshielded 13-pounder (3-inch) anti-aircraft gun on a high-angle mounting

Awning stanchions, normally removed and stowed at sea but displayed on this 'as-fitted' model

Main mast

W/T aerials rigged fr the highest point of t fore mast to achieve maximum range

Rudder

The two starboard-side propellers. The four shafts were powered by Parsons turbines of 40,000 horsepower producing a maximum sea speed of 28 knots

Fog-buoys in their ready-use stowages

Ensign staff. The White Ensign was usually hoisted here when in harbour but a smaller ensign was flown from a gaff on the main mast at sea. In action several White Ensigns, known as Battle Ensigns, were hoisted so that if any one of them was shot away it could not be construed as the ship striking its colours in surrender

Bilge keel to reduce the amount roll to make the ship a better gun platform. Above this the hull was protected by a 2-inch belt over 1-inch plating amidships, with 1-inch plating over the machinery spaces

Single 4-inch guns in open shields; replaced in 1916 by one 6-inch gun on the forecastle and another amidships

as completed in December 1914, which clearly shows how she was designed for a specific purpose. The flared forecastle and hydrodynamic bow allowed her to use her high speed to drive into a rough sea and the large number of light, quick-firing guns mounted forward were intended to facilitate her role as a 'destroyer-killer', defending the Grand Fleet against enemy torpedo-craft in a close range melee. The small, armoured conning tower just forward of the bridge would have given the captain some protection during such a fight but his situational awareness, viewing the action through the narrow slits, would have been minimal. The high forecastle, breakwater aft of the cable deck and gun shields would have given the forward guns' crews some protection against the elements but, with ammunition supplied and loaded by hand, serving the guns in any sort of sea state would not have been work for the weak or faint-hearted. The Director of Naval Construction originally thought that these vessels would be too lively to use 6-inch guns effectively but wartime experience proved that the after guns could be used and their heavier weight of shell was more effective against the larger destroyers being built by the Germans. *Caroline* was re-armed with an all 6-inch main armament in 1916.

Paired 24-inch searchlights for illuminating targets at night and signalling

Fore mast with yardarms for signal flag groups

Principal 12-foot rangefinder

Mechanical semaphore arms for close-range tactical signalling

Forecastle breakwater intended to prevent seawater that washed over the deck in rough weather from interfering with the guns' crews and their ammunition supply party which passed shells from hand to hand

Compass platform with compass binnacle visible at its foremost part

Primary steering position (wheelhouse) and chartroom

Armoured conning tower

Anchor cables running from the cable-holders to the anchors which were securely lashed in their hawsepipes. The deck under the cables was protected by steel plates known as 'scotchmen'

Guardrails; usually kept up at sea but lowered in action so that they did not foul the guns' arcs of fire.

Starboard anchor; there was a similar anchor on the port side

Jack staff – the Union Jack was hoisted when the first line was passed ashore or the first anchor touched bottom

Hydrodynamic underwater bow design

Flared hull design to keep water and spray off the forecastle as much as possible

GERMAN LIGHT CRUISERS

From about 1900 the Imperial German Navy had built a series of light cruisers which were named after cities. The earlier designs were smaller than the British 'Towns', but whereas the Royal Navy then moved to smaller light cruisers, the trend in Germany was the reverse. Originally the German navy regarded volume of fire as more important than the destructive effect of individual shells and the standard armament was ten (later twelve) 10.5cm (4.1-inch) guns. It was not until the eve of the war that the need for a more powerful 15cm (5.9in) gun was accepted, in response to the 6-inch guns in Royal Navy light cruisers.

SLR0015 This model of *Dresden* is a fine example of a German builder's model made in the metric 1/50 scale. She was one of the earlier designs of light cruiser, completed in 1909. Built by Blohm & Voss in Hamburg, who also made the model, she was the first German light cruiser to be fitted with Parsons direct-drive turbines. Her sister-ship *Emden* was sunk by *Sydney* off the Cocos islands in 1914. The model is finished in the German tropical paint scheme with a white hull and buff bridge, masts and funnels. Rigging is well executed and there is a small searchlight mounted on the pole foremast above the bridge although the ship was not adequately equipped for a full night action. Doors and hatches are drawn onto their relevant surfaces and there is a pronounced breakwater on the forecastle aft of the anchors and cables to protect the forward guns' crews against water washing down the deck in rough weather. *Dresden* was stationed in the West Indies before the war and in 1914 she moved into the South Atlantic to attack British

merchant shipping. After rounding Cape Horn she joined the German Asiatic Squadron and took part in the Battle of Coronel in which the British cruisers *Monmouth* and *Good Hope* were sunk. A month later she was the only German cruiser to escape from the Battle of the Falkland Islands, after which she hid among the islands in Chile's complicated coastline until March 1915 when she was located by RN ships and hoisted a white flag of surrender. Using protracted negotiations as cover, her ship's company abandoned *Dresden* and scuttled her. This model was donated to the National Maritime Museum by the Naval War Trophies Committee in 1945.

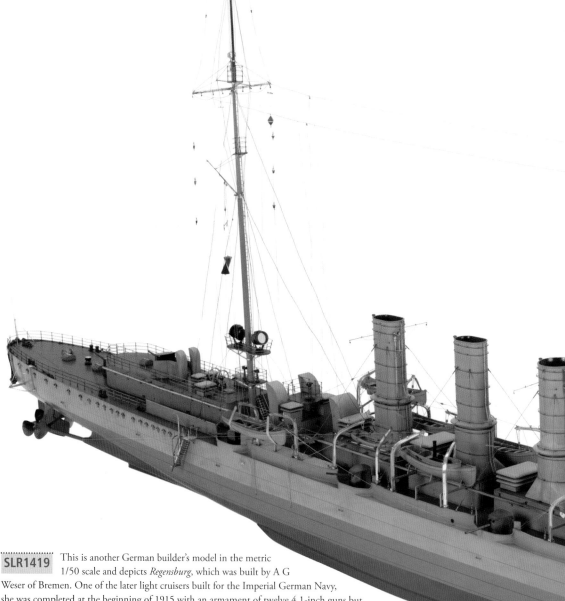

SLR1419 This is another German builder's model in the metric
1/50 scale and depicts *Regensburg*, which was built by A G
Weser of Bremen. One of the later light cruisers built for the Imperial German Navy,
she was completed at the beginning of 1915 with an armament of twelve 4.1-inch guns but
when this was found to be inadequate to engage British light cruisers successfully she was re-armed
with seven 5.9-inch low-angle and two 8.8cm (3.4-inch) high-angle anti-aircraft guns. She was fitted with four
19.7-inch torpedo tubes and rails to carry and lay 120 mines. Two shafts with turbine machinery developing 32,000
horsepower gave her a speed of 27 knots. She spent the whole war with the High Seas Fleet and was present at Jutland. In 1920 she
was handed over to the French Navy as a war reparation and appropriately re-named *Strasbourg*. She served with the French navy until 1937.
The model is highly detailed and makes an interesting comparison with the equivalent British builders' models. It is intended to present a
realistic rather than striking impression and the modelmaker has taken care to produce a life-like effect, especially in the weathered wooden
deck planks. It shows the ship as she appeared when completed with twelve 4.1-inch guns spaced at intervals along the ship's sides from the
forecastle aft and two on the centreline aft. The paint finish is carefully weathered with the correct tones for the period and the treatment of
the glazed scuttles is especially convincing. Two boats are turned out on their davits but not yet lowered and both port and starboard ladders
have been lowered from the forward sections of the quarterdeck. Note that by 1914 the ram bow had been discarded and she has a 'clipper'
bow, cut away below the waterline. The rigging is finely and carefully executed. This exceptional model was donated to the National
Maritime Museum by the Naval War Trophies Committee in 1945.

GUNS AND GUN MOUNTINGS

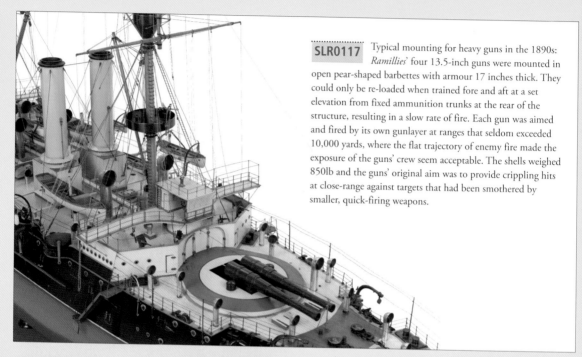

SLR0117 Typical mounting for heavy guns in the 1890s: *Ramillies'* four 13.5-inch guns were mounted in open pear-shaped barbettes with armour 17 inches thick. They could only be re-loaded when trained fore and aft at a set elevation from fixed ammunition trunks at the rear of the structure, resulting in a slow rate of fire. Each gun was aimed and fired by its own gunlayer at ranges that seldom exceeded 10,000 yards, where the flat trajectory of enemy fire made the exposure of the guns' crew seem acceptable. The shells weighed 850lb and the guns' original aim was to provide crippling hits at close-range against targets that had been smothered by smaller, quick-firing weapons.

SLR1408 Open barbettes were soon covered by an armoured hood, which became known as turrets. This shows *Queen Mary's* two forward Mark II* turrets, each of which had two 13.5-inch Mark V guns. The armour on the turret faces was 9 inches thick, 2 inches less than a contemporary battleship. There was a considerable rotating structure under the turrets through which ammunition and silk bags of cordite were supplied to the guns, allowing a rate of fire of about one round per minute. At their greatest elevation of 20 degrees these guns had a maximum range of 23,820 yards and shells weighed 1400lb, nearly double that of the 12-inch.

SLR0117 *Iron Duke's* after Mark II** turrets with their 13.5-inch guns. 'X' turret has deflection scales painted on it and there is a range 'clock' on the after conning tower, devices developed during the War in order to allow the ships of a squadron to concentrate their fire on a selected target. Note the after 6-inch casemate just forward of the accommodation ladder; the gun has been removed because it was too close to the waterline and its opening has been blanked off. The sighting hoods, intended to allow the main armament to be aimed and fired in local control after the ship had received significant damage, stand out prominently in this view.

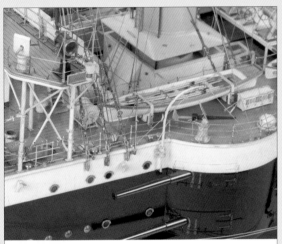

SLR1326 The forward single 9.2-inch Mark V turret in the armoured cruiser *Leviathan*; with the 7.5-inch, also mounted in some armoured cruisers, these were the smallest calibres regularly mounted in fully enclosed gunhouses. The Mark X gun fired a 380lb shell out to a maximum range of 15,000 yards but with no fire control system and guns aimed visually by the gunlayer, hits at anything like this distance would be extremely unlikely. An identical turret was mounted aft.

SLR1326 Two of *Leviathan*'s 6-inch guns in their casemates. Positioning these guns one over the other was intended to reduce the hull length required to mount them but the idea proved unsuccessful because the lower casemates were too close to the waterline and easily flooded. At 100lb, 6-inch shells were the heaviest that could be loaded by hand and *Leviathan* had sixteen to maintain a high, short-range rate of fire against an opponent, although the theoretical maximum range was 14,000 yards. Like the larger guns, they were aimed by gunlayers.

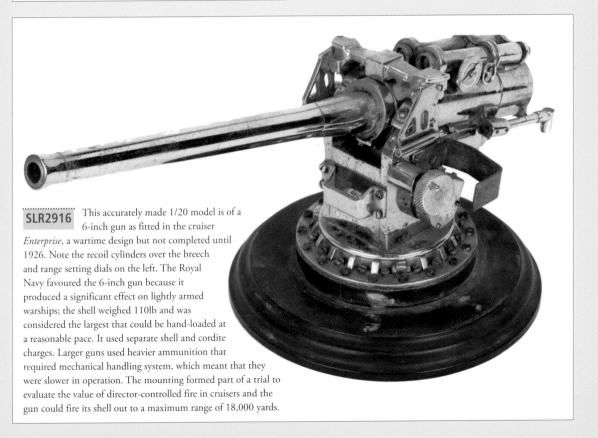

SLR2916 This accurately made 1/20 model is of a 6-inch gun as fitted in the cruiser *Enterprise*, a wartime design but not completed until 1926. Note the recoil cylinders over the breech and range setting dials on the left. The Royal Navy favoured the 6-inch gun because it produced a significant effect on lightly armed warships; the shell weighed 110lb and was considered the largest that could be hand-loaded at a reasonable pace. It used separate shell and cordite charges. Larger guns used heavier ammunition that required mechanical handling system, which meant that they were slower in operation. The mounting formed part of a trial to evaluate the value of director-controlled fire in cruisers and the gun could fire its shell out to a maximum range of 18,000 yards.

SLR2916 A rear view of *Enterprise*'s 6-inch gun at maximum elevation showing the breech closed and the shield usually fitted. The semi-enclosed mounting reflected wartime experience that guns' crews worked more effectively if shielded from the elements.

SLR2932 A 1/12 scale model of the 4.7-inch Mark I quick-firing gun on its CP Mark VI* mounting as used in the later 'W' class, the largest and most effective gun fitted to Royal Navy destroyers in the First World War. It fired a 50lb shell out to a maximum range of 15,000 yards and was ideal for use in the type of fast, close-range action against fleeting targets that First World War destroyers excelled in. It normally had a splinter shield to protect the gun's crew and a single-lever breech control that enabled a rate of fire up to twelve rounds per minute with a fresh crew.

SLR1436 The anti-submarine patrol vessel *P 34*'s single 4-inch gun mounted on the 'bandstand' forward of the bridge. It has a splinter shield for the crew's upper bodies and could fire a 31lb shell out to a maximum range of 11,400 yards. It fired fixed ammunition with the shell attached to the brass cartridge case in order to ease loading and a number of rounds would have been kept near the mounting in ready-use lockers so that it could be brought into action quickly.

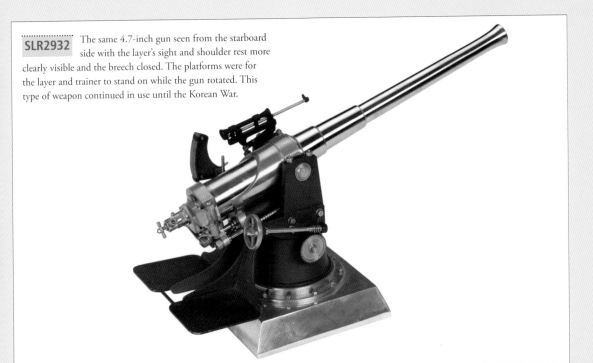

SLR2932 The same 4.7-inch gun seen from the starboard side with the layer's sight and shoulder rest more clearly visible and the breech closed. The platforms were for the layer and trainer to stand on while the gun rotated. This type of weapon continued in use until the Korean War.

SLR0015 The group of five 12-pounder guns mounted aft in the scout cruiser *Forward*. As a scout for the battle fleet she was expected to become involved in a close-quarter melee with ships performing a similar function for the enemy. On completion, therefore, she was armed with ten quick-firing 12-pounders mounted in groups of five forward and aft. The weapon fired a shell that actually weighed 12.5lb out to a maximum range of 11,000 yards. The mountings were unprotected, leaving their crews exposed to the elements and enemy fire, hand-worked and aimed by their individual gunlayers. By 1914 these weapons were considered too light for a cruiser and she had been re-armed with nine 4-inch and a single 3-inch anti-aircraft gun.

SLR1436 A 2-pounder 'pom-pom' Mark II automatic cannon fitted to *P 34* amidships to give rapid fire against small vessels, aircraft and surfaced U-boats. The basic gun had been introduced in 1892 but this version used the more recent high-angle Mark II mounting for anti-aircraft use. Shells weighed 2lb and were fed into the weapon by a 35-round belt giving a cyclic rate of fire of 200 rounds per minute. The ammunition was fixed and each round weighed 2.95lb with the propellant so the boxes containing belted rounds were not easy to bring to the mounting. The box for the belt was attached to the right-hand side of the gun but has not been fitted in this model. Maximum range was 6900 yards and the gun was usually fired in bursts of 5 rounds.

5: Destroyers

In the late nineteenth century only another capital ship could disable and sink a battleship but this changed after the invention of the self-propelled, or locomotive, torpedo by the British engineer Robert Whitehead in 1868. The new weapon could be launched from small, fast vessels and hit their targets below the waterline with a large explosive charge capable of causing lethal damage. Torpedo boats were little more than launches at first and could be built in large numbers to tilt the balance of naval power away from the battleship and make close blockade a dangerous and expensive option. From the mid-1880s the Royal Navy attempted to produce a counter to this threat in the form of torpedo gunboats – sometimes called 'catchers' – which were essentially scaled-down cruisers, intended primarily to protect the fleet from torpedo attack. They proved inadequate, not being fast enough, but they continued to be built into the 1890s, including a number for export.

Great Britain was the world leader in torpedo-boat development, but the Directorate of Naval Construction itself had little knowledge of small high-speed craft.

Therefore, in 1892 Admiral Fisher, then the Controller responsible for warship construction on the Admiralty Board, asked the heads of two firms that specialised in torpedo-boat construction, John Isaac Thornycroft and Alfred Fernandez Yarrow, to produce plans for a warship to protect the fleet from attack by torpedo boats. The vessels that resulted were effectively enlarged versions of the craft they were intended to counter and were named, in true Fisher style, torpedo-boat destroyers or TBDs. In time they were referred to simply as destroyers.

SLR1275 British firms built large numbers of torpedo-armed vessels for export and the Chilean *Almirante Simpson* was designed and built by Laird's in 1896. Similar to the RN *Dryad* class torpedo gunboats, her design was soon overtaken by the new 'destroyers' such as *Whiting*. This 1/48 scale builder's model has a wealth of detail including the searchlight mounting on the bridge, which has a glass lens, and the ready-use shells stacked near the guns. Boats on the port side davits are turned out ready for lowering; those on the starboard side turned inboard and secured for sea. The single torpedo tube on the starboard side is turned out into its launch position, the port mounting is stowed fore and aft. She was expected to take part in a close-quarter action at high speed and reflects RN thinking at the time by having a reinforced ram bow with a single, forward-facing torpedo tube above it. Machinery comprised four coal-fired Normand boilers and two-shaft triple-expansion engines delivering 4500 horsepower and 21 knots in ideal conditions with good quality coal. Gun armament comprised two 4.7-inch and four 3-pounder weapons in addition to the three 18-inch torpedo tubes. Sold by Chile to Ecuador in 1907, she proved popular with her new owners and continued in service with them until 1935.

TORPEDO-BOAT DESTROYERS

Destroyers were larger than torpedo boats with high speed, greater radius of action and a quick-firing gun armament in addition to torpedoes. They were intended to protect the battle fleet against torpedo attack and to fulfil all the functions of torpedo boats themselves, rendering the earlier type obsolete by 1914. The first prototypes were *Havock* and *Hornet* from Yarrow together with *Daring* and *Decoy* from Thornycroft, completed in 1894-5. The pattern adopted for future construction involved a broad specification laid down by the Admiralty translated into specific design details and drawings by individual shipbuilders. Early destroyers had coal-fired boilers, reciprocating machinery and were capable of 26 knots in calm conditions. Displacement was about 200 tons and armament comprised a single 12-pounder gun forward and a 6-pounder aft with one or two torpedo tubes. Large orders followed: the first series were generically termed '27-knotters' from their design speed, but these were soon succeeded by '30-knotters'. Progress was rapid with the first turbine-powered destroyers, *Viper* and *Cobra*, capable of speeds up to 35 knots, delivered in 1899.

Torpedo tubes were built into the bow of the first ships so that they could be aimed directly at the target but they proved difficult to use and caused spray over the bridge. A better arrangement was found to be the installation of single, trainable tubes until later in the First World War when twin and eventually triple mountings became common so that destroyers could carry out co-ordinated, massed torpedo attacks on the enemy. The first destroyers were given traditional gunboat names but as large classes evolved, they were given names with a common theme, the first being the 'River' class.

SLR1273 *Whiting*, a '30-knotter', was built by Palmers
Shipbuilding & Iron Company at Jarrow-on-Tyne
and completed in 1897. This 1/48 scale model was made by the
builder and shows some of the principal features associated with the
early destroyers, including the 'turtleback' bow intended to keep
spray clear of the after deck, and the 12-pounder gun mounted on
top of the conning tower where it had a good arc of fire. Two-shaft
machinery gave a top speed of 30 knots in calm conditions. She had
four boilers with the central two back-to-back so that their uptakes
could be trunked together, hence the larger second funnel. In service
the forward gun platform was used as a bridge and a painted canvas
'dodger' would have been fitted around the guardrails to act as a
windbreak. She deployed to the China Station in 1897 and
remained there until sold for scrap in 1919.

Thirty-six 'River' class destroyers were built from 1903 onwards, representing a significant advance in design that sacrificed absolute speed for better sea-keeping qualities. Displacement grew to 620 tons and the 'turtleback' bow was replaced by a raised forecastle, a design feature that became standard in British destroyers for the next half-century. They had coal-burning boilers and machinery of 7000 horsepower gave a sustainable speed of just over 25 knots. The designed armament was a single 12-pounder gun forward with three 6-pounders on the iron deck aft, mounted in different positions by the different builders. Two single, trainable torpedo tubes were mounted; one between the funnels and one further aft; reload torpedoes could be carried on the upper deck.

SLR0114 An unusually large 1/32 scale builder's model of the 'River' class destroyer *Boyne* shows the raised forecastle and small bridge typical of the class, with a searchlight mounted over the bridge to give them a night-fighting capability. Detailed design to meet the Admiralty specification was the responsibility of her builder, Hawthorn Leslie & Co of Hebburn-on-Tyne. Prominent ventilators close to the funnels allowed air to be drawn into the boilers, and a 27-foot Montague whaler, ready for immediate use as a sea-boat, can be seen attached to davits on the port side aft. The scuttles in the raised forecastle and right aft show the accommodation areas, with the machinery installation amidships filling the entire width of the hull. There was no passage through the engine and boiler rooms and all movement had to be via the upper deck, which could be washed down in rough seas. She served on the China Station before 1914 and was subsequently used as a convoy escort in both the Mediterranean and the North Sea before being withdrawn from service and sold for scrap in 1919.

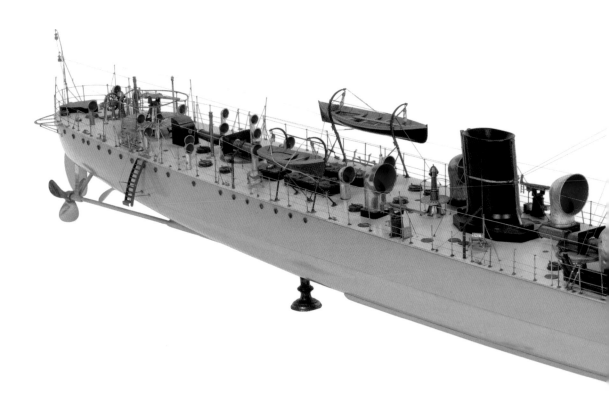

THE FIRST 'TRIBAL' CLASS

The next evolutionary step came in 1904 when the Admiralty specified larger destroyers with oil-fired boilers capable of 33 knots and able to steam at full power for eight hours in a moderate sea. At first the builders were to be given a completely free hand to interpret the requirement, but when their initial bids showed radically different designs, DNC insisted on firmer guidance being laid down. The resulting destroyers evolved into the 'Tribal' class, with turbine machinery but differing types and numbers of boilers to give the required steam pressure.

SLR1380 *Ghurka* was a 'Tribal' class destroyer built by Hawthorn Leslie & Co of Hebburn-on-Tyne, who also made this 1/48 scale model. She was completed in 1907 with the name spelt as shown; the next vessel to bear the name was another destroyer (of the second 'Tribal' class), but in her case it was spelt 'Gurkha'. The first British destroyer design to exceed 1000 tons, they had machinery of 14,250 horsepower to maintain a speed of 33 knots in moderate seas. This model gives a good idea of *Ghurka*'s layout. She was armed with three 12-pounder guns, two of which were at the after end of the forecastle to give the maximum weight of fire forward as the ship advanced to counter an enemy torpedo attack or to deliver one of its own. Two single, trainable torpedo tubes were mounted on the iron deck aft and ammunition racks can be seen around the after gun mounting. *Ghurka* was lost off Dungeness on 8 February 1917 when she struck a German mine; only five of her ship's company survived.

REVERSION TO COAL-FIRING

One final class of coal-fired destroyers was produced because of fears that the supply of furnace fuel oil might become limited in wartime. The *Beagle* or 'G' class of sixteen vessels had a displacement slightly greater than the preceding 'Tribal' class, but the reversion to coal meant that the ship's company had to be increased by an extra 35 stokers. They were the first class fitted for 21-inch torpedo tubes, although these were still single mountings, and the gun armament was increased to a single 4-inch mounted on the forecastle and three 12-pounders mounted on the iron deck aft. Her 14,000 horsepower gave a maximum speed of 27 knots but like all other coal-burning ships, the actual top speed depended on the quality of coal and the skill of the stokers. They were the first destroyers to be fitted with stockless anchors, and *Grasshopper* cost £107,884 to build. The *Beagle*s were the last British

destroyers built to drawings prepared by individual shipbuilders with considerable latitude allowable provided that the Staff Requirement was met. Later classes were built to Admiralty designs now that their construction was better understood by the DNC and his Department.

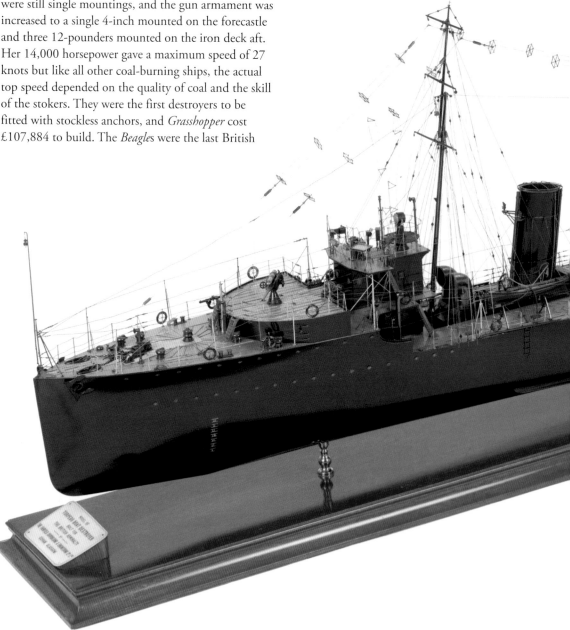

SLR1391 This 1/48 scale model of *Grasshopper* was made in Fairfield's own modelmaking workshop at Govan to show their own version of the *Beagle* class design and it was displayed at shipbuilding exhibitions in Turin in 1911 and Glasgow as late as 1931. The dark paintwork is representative of the ship's early appearance, but the gold-plated fittings were intended to look striking. The rigging is particularly well portrayed and the wireless telegraphy aerials were made from fine copper wire. Both single torpedo tubes are visible, one right aft and the second just forward of the after gun mounting. The after mounting was found to be difficult to operate and the positioning was not repeated. She had a reasonable outfit of boats for her size with two 27-foot whalers and two 24-foot gigs carried on davits and one 13.5-foot dinghy stowed on deck. The degree of skill with which the model was finished is typified by the chart table on the small bridge, on which a miniature chart of the North Sea has been placed. *Grasshopper* was laid down in April 1909 and completed in July 1910. She served throughout the First World War and was withdrawn from service and broken up for scrap in 1921. Three *Beagle*s were lost during the war.

ADMIRALTY DESIGNS

Next came the twenty ships of the *Acorn* or 'H' class, followed in turn by the *Acheron* or 'I' class of twenty-three ships. All reverted to oil-fired boilers and were built to an Admiralty design except for nine modified as 'specials' by Yarrow, Thornycroft and Palmers. Externally similar, they had increased horsepower to achieve greater speed. The basic *Acheron*s had 13,500 horsepower giving a realistic sea speed of 27 knots. The ultimate 'special' was *Oak*, built by Yarrow, which had machinery of 20,000 horsepower to achieve a speed of 32 knots. For much of the First World War she acted as a tender to the Grand Fleet flagship and embarked His Majesty King George V during his visits to the Fleet in Scapa Flow. They had a ship's company of 71 and were armed with two 4-inch and two 12-pounder guns. Two single, trainable torpedo launchers were mounted on the centreline aft of the after funnel with a searchlight mounted on a 'bandstand' between them to facilitate night action. The three boilers were mounted with the forward two back-to-back so that their exhaust could be trunked through the larger, forward funnel. Smoke from the third boiler was discharged through the smaller, after funnel. Unusually, these ships had three shafts. They were the first destroyers to be fitted with Parsons geared turbines to improve their cruising performance.

SLR0103 *Jackal*, of the 'I' class, was built by Hawthorn Leslie, completed in September 1911, and this 1/48 scale model was made by her builder. Fine details include the tread plates around the capstan to help sailors raise anchor by hand after a mechanical capstan failure. There is a 4-inch gun on the forecastle with a second right aft. The two 12-pounder guns are sited aft of the forecastle break where they would be protected when the ship was steaming fast into a rough sea. The motor boat is suspended from the starboard davits and the whaler to port. Two replacement torpedoes are on deck between the tubes, and searchlights are mounted over the bridge and in a 'bandstand' between the torpedo tubes for night-fighting. There is a mechanical semaphore arm on the starboard side of the bridge and the upper deck is fitted with both guardrails and awning supports. Note the torpedo davits to port and starboard amidships, used to hoist torpedoes inboard and to help load them into the tubes. *Jackal* and her sister-ship *Hornet* carried out a remarkable rescue in October 1915 when the cruiser *Argyll* was wrecked on the Bell Rock. They managed to get alongside the stricken cruiser, one at a time, in a severe gale to take off her entire ship's company. Prior to that *Jackal* had served with the 1st Destroyer Flotilla at the Battle of Dogger Bank in January 1915. She later transferred to the Mediterranean Fleet and fought against Austrian destroyers during an action in the Straits of Otranto in April 1918. She was hit twice by shellfire and damaged. Seven of her sister-ships became war losses and *Jackal*, together with the other surviving members of the class, was sold for scrap in 1920.

TOWARDS A STANDARD DESTROYER

The 'M' class were the last pre-war destroyer design. Thirteen were ordered in the first batch, and a large number of repeat vessels were ordered under War Emergency Programmes, with names beginning with the letters 'M', 'N'. 'O' and 'P'. The later 'R' class were slightly improved versions of the 'M's with geared turbines making them more efficient and economical 'steamers'. Externally the only differences were larger shields for the 4-inch guns with the after mounting placed on a 'bandstand' to give some protection against water and spray. The forecastle was raised by a foot and extended slightly further aft with increased flare to improve sea-worthiness in rough weather. They were succeeded by the modified 'R' and 'S' classes with names beginning with 'R', 'S', 'T' and 'U'. The 'S' class continued in production when it was learnt that the Germans were not building large destroyers in significant numbers and the Grand Fleet did not, therefore, need all its destroyers to be as large as the later 'V' and 'W' classes. Some of the early 'S' class had fixed athwartship torpedo tubes aft of the forecastle break but these proved difficult to aim and they reverted to the more practical rotatable mounts.

The 'M' class formed the backbone of the Grand Fleet destroyer flotillas until 1917. There were slight variations between ships from different builders but the majority displaced about 1000 tons at deep load and had an armament of three 4-inch quick-firing guns, with stowage for 120 rounds per gun, and two single 2-pounder pom-poms, each with 1000 rounds per gun; the latter were intended for use against both air and close-range surface targets. For the first time double torpedo tubes were fitted in two trainable mountings, giving a 'broadside' of four 21-inch torpedoes. Following the destruction of a U-boat when it was rammed by the destroyer *Badger* in October 1914, all destroyers had a sharp, square ram stem fitted with stiffened structure around it to facilitate similar offensive action. The Thornycroft vessels had two-shaft machinery of 26,500 horsepower giving a design speed of 35 knots. One of these, *Mastiff*, exceeded the designed horsepower by 6860 on trials and reached just over 37 knots on a light displacement and 34 on a deep displacement, but furnace fuel oil consumption was excessive at these speeds. In 1915 she had the reputation of being the fastest ship in the Royal Navy. Thornycroft ships had four boilers with the centre two back-to-back exhausting through shared uptakes; the centre funnel was, thus, larger than the other two. The officers' and engine room artificers' accommodation was right aft and the sailors' forward in the raised forecastle.

FEATURES OF A DESTROYER

SLR0110 Destroyers were used by the Grand Fleet for a number of purposes, as a screening force for the battle fleet and as striking forces based at Harwich and Dover. Admiral Jellicoe never felt that he had enough destroyers and pessimistically believed the Germans to have 88 at the Battle of Jutland on 31 May 1916. In fact they only had 58, far fewer than the British total of 80. By 1914 the destroyer had virtually supplanted the torpedo boat in the Royal Navy and taken over its functions as well as fulfilling its primary task as a 'torpedo-boat killer'. This 1/48 scale model of *Mastiff*, one of the numerically large 'M' class, was made by the ship's builders, Thornycroft, and shows her as completed in September 1914. It demonstrates all the qualities of the wartime destroyer, with quick-firing guns sited to give all-round fire, twin trainable torpedo tubes and a light anti-aircraft armament. Small 24-inch searchlights gave a limited night-fighting capability. The guns were fired by their gunlayers over open sights and were intended principally for fast action at close range. Ammunition was passed to the guns by 'human chains' over the upper deck from the magazines, and rough weather would have caused a reduction in the rate of fire. There was no protection for guns' crews or handling parties in action. The torpedoes were aimed from the bridge.

Fore mast with yardarms for signal flag groups

Bridge – in service painted canvas 'dodgers' would have been fitted over the guardrails to give some protection against wind and spray

Forward 20-inch searchlight

Compass binnacle

Structure containing the wheelhouse, chartroom and wireless telegraphy office

Forward single 4-inch gun

Awning stanchion; normally only rigged in harbour when needed

Starboard anchor cable

Starboard cable 'bonnet'

Jack staff

Capstan

Port anchor secured in its hawsepipe

Port anchor cable

Raised, flared forecastle designed to improve the ship's sea-keeping qualities at high speed in rough seas

'Bonnet' over the port navel pipe intended to prevent sea water spilling down into the cable locker

She was capable of 35 knots in a calm sea and the
raised forecastle and midships 'bandstand' would have
kept her guns largely clear of wash and spray. The torpedo tubes and after gun would have been more sus-
ceptible to water washing down the iron deck.

After 4-inch quick-firing Mark IV gun on a
P.IX mounting. *Mastiff* had stowage in her
magazines for 360 rounds for these guns

W/T (wireless telegraphy) aerials rigged
between the fore and main masts

Mechanical semaphore arm to port
of the searchlight

Main mast

Ensign staff

20-foot motor boat on quadrantal
davits, secured for sea by crossed
gripes

Siren

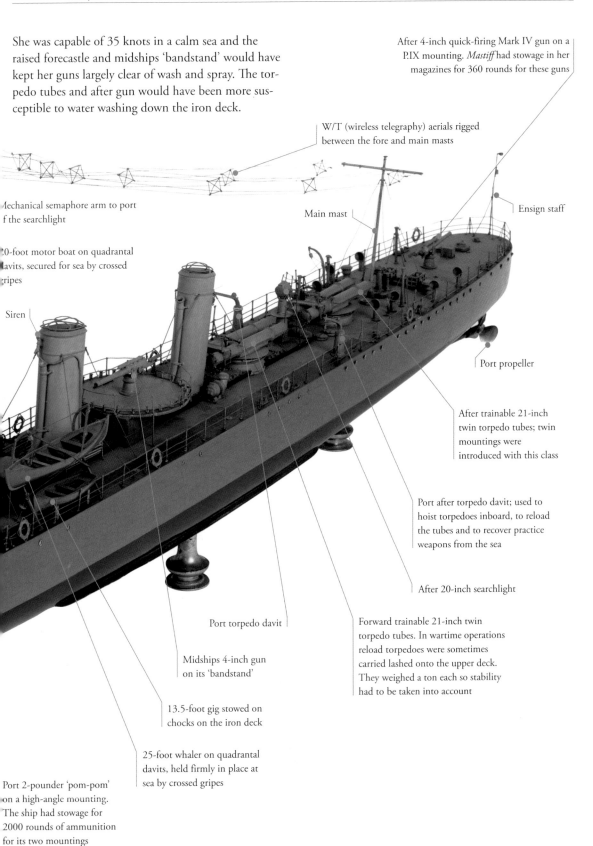

Port propeller

After trainable 21-inch
twin torpedo tubes; twin
mountings were
introduced with this class

Port after torpedo davit; used to
hoist torpedoes inboard, to reload
the tubes and to recover practice
weapons from the sea

After 20-inch searchlight

Port torpedo davit

Midships 4-inch gun
on its 'bandstand'

Forward trainable 21-inch twin
torpedo tubes. In wartime operations
reload torpedoes were sometimes
carried lashed onto the upper deck.
They weighed a ton each so stability
had to be taken into account

13.5-foot gig stowed on
chocks on the iron deck

25-foot whaler on quadrantal
davits, held firmly in place at
sea by crossed gripes

Port 2-pounder 'pom-pom'
on a high-angle mounting.
The ship had stowage for
2000 rounds of ammunition
for its two mountings

THE 'V&W's

The Royal Navy's ultimate First World War destroyers were the 'V' and 'W' classes, which evolved from a group of five ships originally intended to act as flotilla leaders. The requirement specified the same 26,000 horsepower machinery as the 'R' class and a sea-speed of 34 knots, but their heavier armament and greater endurance required more ammunition, fuel and feed water, which increased their displacement. Hull length was saved, however, by adopting superfiring gun mountings in 'B' and 'X' positions and only two funnels – tall and thin forward for a single boiler and short and fat aft for the other two boilers mounted back-to-back (although this was reversed in later ships to improve watertight integrity). This arrangement allowed the bridge to be moved further aft and a larger, more flared forecastle. Repeat 'V's and 'W's were ordered in several batches, not all of which were completed by the Armistice, but they were generally regarded as a single 'V&W' class. The first batch had four 4-inch guns which fired a 31lb shell with a maximum range of 10,000 yards although, with no director, hits at this range would be unlikely. By 1917 war experience showed that hits with these shells were unlikely to disable a destroyer unless they damaged its machinery. Later 'V&W's were, therefore, armed with 4.7-inch guns which fired a 50lb shell and earlier ships were re-armed as the opportunity arose. Earlier ships had two twin, rotatable 21-inch torpedo tubes but later ones mounted triple tubes. Some were

modified to act as fleet minesweepers with the sweep gear replacing the after gun and depth charge fittings. The 'V&W's were one of the best warship designs of all time and formed the basis of British and many foreign navies' destroyer designs for a further three decades.

There were some differences between the destroyers from the various builders but they all conformed to a standard Admiralty design. They were 312 feet long overall with a beam just under 30 feet. Deep displacement was 1490 tons. Two-shaft machinery of 27,000 horsepower gave a speed of 34 knots and an endurance of 2600 miles at 15 knots. At full power the radius dropped dramatically to only 600 miles, so high speed had to be used sparingly. In addition to the four main guns, most ships had a single 3-inch anti-aircraft gun. All the ships were given names beginning with 'V' or 'W', although a few of the cancelled ships were allocated 'Y' and 'Z' names.

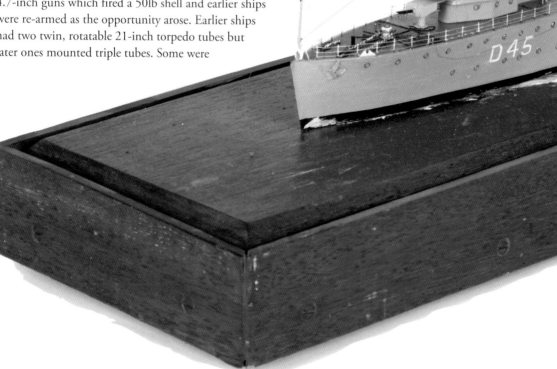

SLR1445 The first group of 'W's were repeat 'V's but with triple torpedo tubes. *Westminster*, one of this group, was built by Scott's Shipbuilding and Engineering Company of Greenock on the Clyde and was launched on 24 February 1918. This 1/192 scale waterline model of was made in 1960 and depicts her under way after 1918. Despite its small size, it is well detailed and the paint scheme shows the ship as she would have appeared in service. The 4-inch guns have shields fitted to protect their crews against shrapnel and sea spray while in action. A whaler, rigged as a sea-boat, is suspended from the port davits and a motor boat from the starboard. The single anti-aircraft gun is mounted on a 'bandstand' abaft the after funnel and torpedo davits are clearly visible on either side of the hull between the two torpedo mountings where they could be used to bring reloads inboard in harbour, recover practice torpedoes from the water and reload the

tubes themselves. A small 'bandstand between the tubes has a searchlight mounted for night fighting. The black chimneys visible aft of the bridge and on the after superstructure carried away the exhaust gases from the coal-fired galley ranges; they appear to be a little too large for the scale of the model but their inclusion adds interest. The model is rigged realistically with wireless telegraphy aerials running aft from the fore mast to the diminutive main mast. A jack staff is in place forward and an ensign staff aft indicating that the ship has just left, or is about to enter, harbour but the White Ensign is flying from the main. *Westminster* survived to see service in the Second World War, re-armed for use as an anti-aircraft escort destroyer with Western Approaches Command, a type of conversion referred to as a 'Wair'. She was not finally withdrawn from service until 1945 and was eventually scrapped at Rosyth in August 1948.

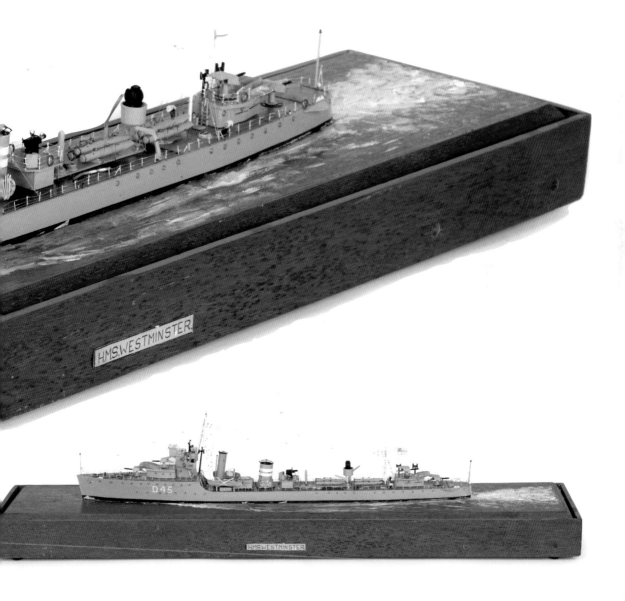

SLR1446 This model of *Warwick* is also to 1/192 scale and was made by Norman Ough in, or before, 1932. It is a waterline model showing the ship as she was in 1918, moored to a buoy but it is not mounted on a sea-scape. This view shows the 4-inch gun mountings and their shields to advantage, together with the triple torpedo tubes and the single anti-aircraft gun in a 'bandstand' abaft the after funnel. The galley funnels are portrayed at a more realistic scale than the previous model, and boats, depth charges and other upper deck fittings are beautifully detailed. *Warwick* was one of the ships which could be modified to act as minelayers and rails were fitted on the port and starboard sides running aft from the boat davits to the angled ramps at the stern from which they were dropped. Each rail could carry 30 Mark VIII mines with their sinkers acting as wheeled trolleys on which they moved along the rails. Each destroyer thus fitted could, therefore, carry 60 mines, but individual mines, together with their sinkers

weighed 1840lb and to compensate for the added weight aft 'Y' gun mounting and all its ammunition together with the after torpedo tubes had to be removed. When this happened, it was usual for canvas screens to be rigged with the silhouette of the gun mounting and torpedo tubes painted on them make it look as if the full armament was still in place. *Warwick* is shown with the

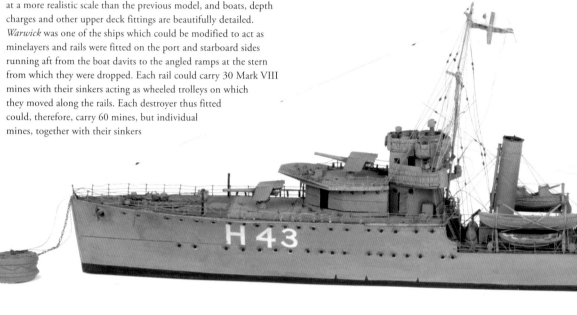

rails in place but no mines and with her full gun and torpedo armament. She was built by Hawthorn Leslie on the Tyne and launched on 28 December 1917. War service was short but interesting and in April 1918 she acted as Admiral Sir Roger Keyes' flagship during the attack on Zeebrugge (note that the model has a Vice Admiral's flag on the fore mast and the White Ensign at the main mast). She took part in the subsequent operation against Ostend but set off a mine which broke her back. Towed back to

Dover by her sister-ship *Velox*, she underwent extensive repairs. She was recommissioned for service in the Second World War, and converted for duty as a long-range escort destroyer. On 20 February, while searching for a submarine twenty miles southwest of Trevose Head in Cornwall, she was hit by a homing torpedo from *U 413* that set off a secondary explosion. She went down in four minutes with the loss of 43 members of her ship's company, but 93 others were rescued.

SLR1448 *Wolverine* was a repeat 'W' class destroyer built by J S White & Co of Cowes on the Isle of Wight, armed with the later outfit of four 4.7-inch guns and triple torpedo tubes. Rather than the single 3-inch, she has two 2-pounder 'pom-poms' as anti-aircraft armament in a 'bandstand' between the funnels. Apart from the heavier main armament, this group could be distinguished by the broader funnel being forward rather than aft and a stern which was straight in profile rather than concave. A rangefinder for the main armament is mounted over the bridge. The model was made by her builder and is to the standard 1/48 scale. She was launched on 17 July

1919, too late for war service, and the model shows her as she appeared on completion. Like many of her sister-ships, *Wolverine* survived to see service in the Second World War, modified for use as a short-range escort destroyer. She earned fame on 17 March 1941 while forming part of the escort for an Atlantic convoy when, in company with the corvettes *Arbutus* and *Camellia*, she sank two U-boats, *U 70* and *U 47*. *U 47* and her commanding officer, Gunther Prien, were famous for sinking the battleship *Royal Oak* in Scapa Flow on 14 October 1939. After her withdrawal from service in 1945, *Wolverine* was broken up at Troon in September 1946.

DESTROYER DEVELOPMENT

COMMAND AND CONTROL

The need for adequate command and control facilities led to increases in the size of the bridge structures in successive classes of destroyer. This is well illustrated by comparing the very basic conning position in *Whiting* (1897) and a still relatively simple arrangement in *Grasshopper* (1910), with the much more sophisticated bridge structure as fitted at the end of the War in *Warwick*.

SLR1391 *Grasshopper*'s model shows that the command arrangements remain very basic and are still entirely open, but the bridge is now larger and raised to offer a better view over the forward gun (the broad platform was originally intended to mount two 12-pounders, although these were replaced by a single 4-inch). There is a chart table to the left of the magnetic compass binnacle and the single 20-inch searchlight at the rear was used to indicate targets to the guns at night. The noise and blast from the forward gun, together with the wind and spray in a high-speed action, would have been significant distractions and, on anything but a clear day that allowed a sextant to be used, the commander's knowledge of his position would have been approximate at best.

SLR1273 Early TBDs like *Whiting* were conned from an extension of the bandstand on which the forward gun was mounted. Navigation equipment was little more than a compass binnacle and ship's wheel, and the only protection was provided by canvas 'dodgers' (not shown on this model) around the guardrails.

SLR1448 By the end of the War, the latest destroyers like *Warwick* had a large enclosed wheelhouse with substantial bridge wings, although there was still an open compass platform above from where the ship was conned. She has a gun director and those equipped as leaders also carried a rangefinder at the rear of the compass platform. There are signal projectors in the bridge wings and all the rails are covered with protective splinter mattresses.

In *Grasshopper* the enlarged machinery spaces took up deck space and forced the single torpedo tubes to be sited further aft, including one right at the stern (a position never repeated). Note the two reloads stowed on deck.

TORPEDO ARMAMENT

The size of a torpedo salvo that could be fired from an individual destroyer grew dramatically in the decade before 1918 because the increasing size of successive classes allowed them to carry more topweight. Illustrated here are the single tubes fitted in *Grasshopper*, the twin tubes in *Mastiff* (1914) and the triple tubes fitted in *Warwick*. In 1914 a typical destroyer could launch two torpedoes, by 1918 a later 'W' class could launch six and a massed attack by destroyers represented a potentially formidable means of engaging an enemy fleet. Massed torpedo attacks by destroyers continued to form an important part of the Royal Navy's doctrine well into the Second World War.

Mastiff's two twin 21-inch torpedo tubes. This class introduced the twin mountings, which became the standard RN destroyer outfit for the rest of the War.

The 'W' class introduced triple torpedo tubes, contrived by fitting a third tube above a standard twin mounting, as shown in this model of *Warwick*.

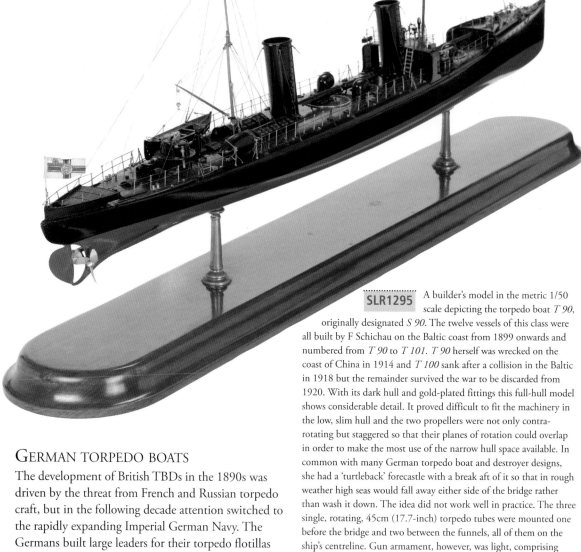

SLR1295 A builder's model in the metric 1/50 scale depicting the torpedo boat *T 90*, originally designated *S 90*. The twelve vessels of this class were all built by F Schichau on the Baltic coast from 1899 onwards and numbered from *T 90* to *T 101*. *T 90* herself was wrecked on the coast of China in 1914 and *T 100* sank after a collision in the Baltic in 1918 but the remainder survived the war to be discarded from 1920. With its dark hull and gold-plated fittings this full-hull model shows considerable detail. It proved difficult to fit the machinery in the low, slim hull and the two propellers were not only contra-rotating but staggered so that their planes of rotation could overlap in order to make the most use of the narrow hull space available. In common with many German torpedo boat and destroyer designs, she had a 'turtleback' forecastle with a break aft of it so that in rough weather high seas would fall away either side of the bridge rather than wash it down. The idea did not work well in practice. The three single, rotating, 45cm (17.7-inch) torpedo tubes were mounted one before the bridge and two between the funnels, all of them on the ship's centreline. Gun armament, however, was light, comprising only three single 50mm (4-pounder) guns, and these ships would have been extremely vulnerable in a surface action by day. Perhaps for this reason, they were relegated to harbour or coastal defence duties before 1914. *T 90* had coal-fired boilers and triple-expansion steam machinery of 5900 horsepower which gave a speed of up to 26 knots in calm conditions. She was 207 feet long and displaced 395 tons, with a ship's company of 60. The model is an accurate representation of these ships, which were painted dark grey or black in expectation of night action. Low in the water, they would have made a difficult gunnery target but their lively motion in anything but a calm sea would have made aiming their torpedoes difficult. This model was presented to the National Maritime Museum by the Naval War Trophies Committee in 1945.

GERMAN TORPEDO BOATS

The development of British TBDs in the 1890s was driven by the threat from French and Russian torpedo craft, but in the following decade attention switched to the rapidly expanding Imperial German Navy. The Germans built large leaders for their torpedo flotillas that they called Division Boats, but they did not possess the speed or firepower of TBDs. Eventually Germany followed the British lead, but even then their TBD equivalents continued to be classed as 'large torpedo boats'. The Germans generally numbered rather than named their torpedo craft, using a system where the initial letter denoted the builder: for example, S for Schichau (Elbing), G for Germaniawerft (Kiel). In 1910 the older torpedo boats were given the new standard T prefix to free the original numbers for allocation to new destroyer-type boats.

SLR1428 This builder's model of the Imperial German Navy destroyer *G 37* was made by Krupp's Germaniawerft at Kiel in the metric 1/50 scale. Ordered in 1914 as a mobilisation design, she was one of six sister-ships numbered *G 37* to *G 42* and was completed in 1915. Roughly comparable to the British 'M' class, they carried a heavier torpedo armament but a weaker gun armament with six 50cm (19.7-inch) torpedo tubes and three 88mm (3.45-inch) guns. The tubes were arranged with one either side of the bridge on fixed mountings and two twin trainable tubes aft of the after funnel on the centreline, separated by a 'bandstand' with a gun on it. At just over 1000 tons they had 25,000 horsepower machinery on twin shafts which gave a speed of up to 36 knots in calm conditions. The model is painted black above the waterline like the ship itself and has gold-plated fittings which stand out against the dark hull and superstructure. This design abandoned the earlier feature of a well-deck before the bridge, but unlike British destroyers the bridge is enclosed and a sea-boat is suspended from a derrick between the funnels rather than from davits. This would have had some advantages but would not have been as practical in rough weather. The structures over the forecastle and quarterdeck are fittings for awnings. This model was transferred to the collection of the National Maritime Museum by the Naval War Trophies Committee in 1945. All six ships of this class fought in the Battle of Jutland. *G 37* herself sank off Walcheren in 1917 after striking a mine. Also in 1917 *G 42* was rammed and sunk by the British destroyer *Broke* near the Goodwin Sands. *G 41* was blown up and abandoned by German forces in Bruges as they retreated in 1918. *G 38*, *G 39* and *G 40* were among the German ships interned in Scapa Flow in 1918. They were scuttled in 1919 and subsequently raised between 1926 and 1928 and sold for scrap, starting with *G 40*.

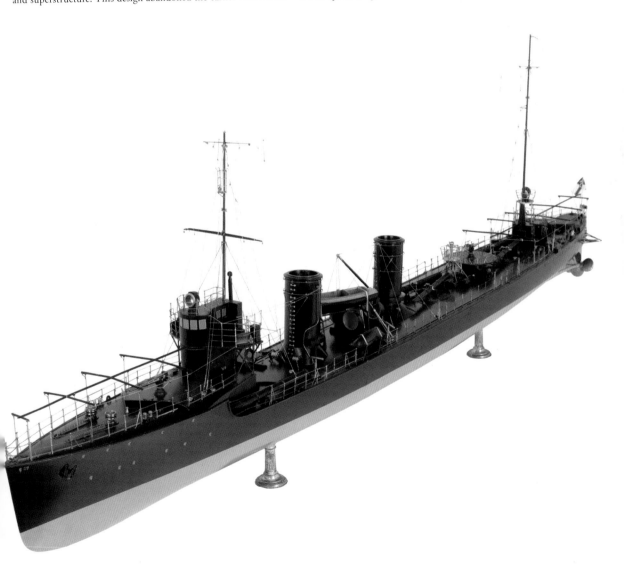

6: Submarines

The first practical submarine was designed by John P Holland, a British migrant to the United States in the last years of the nineteenth century. Effectively a submersible torpedo boat only 63 feet 4 inches long with a displacement of 120 tons on the surface, it had a single 18-inch torpedo tube in the bow and carried four reloads. A single petrol engine gave a maximum speed of 9 knots on the surface and charged a bank of batteries that drove the electric motor when dived. The maximum dived speed was 7 knots but this could only be maintained for a few minutes. An hour was the longest period that the boat could realistically remain dived, and the captain's knowledge of what was happening on

the surface was limited to what he could see through his tiny periscope with its lens only inches above water level. The Admiralty obtained a licence to build boats to Holland's design in 1901, and ordered five boats from Vickers' shipyard at Barrow-in-Furness under an exclusive contract for £35,000 each. They were allocated numbers rather than names and the RN based them at Fort Blockhouse in Gosport to evaluate their potential and to develop anti-submarine tactics for the surface fleet. These early boats were soon overtaken by the development of bigger and better submarines capable of operating outside coastal waters and the first was sold to T W Ward for scrap in 1913.

The last Holland boats were followed by the larger

'A' class, which displaced 204 tons and had a surface speed of 12 knots. Twelve 'A's were followed by eleven 'B's and thirty-eight 'C's between 1906 and 1909. The latter displaced 280 tons and were capable of surface speeds up to 13 knots, but the biggest advance came with the 'D' class built between 1908 and 1911. These introduced external ballast tanks, diesel engines driving twin propellers, bow torpedo tubes placed one above the other and a stern tube. Accommodation was significantly improved and several had a 12-pounder gun fitted so that they could surface to engage a small target without having to waste an expensive torpedo on it. Displacement was 550 tons on the surface and 620 tons dived, and they had a surface speed of 16 knots with up to 10 knots from the electric motors when dived. By 1908 the Admiralty sought to diversify submarine construction, limited up to then by the exclusive contract with Vickers, and the last two 'D's and the first two of the subsequent 'E's were built by Chatham Dockyard.

SLR0111 This 1/24 scale model of *Holland 1* was made by Vickers in November 1962 for presentation to Rear Admiral H S Mackenzie DSO DSC, who was Flag Officer Submarines at the time and about to become the Chief Executive of the Polaris Submarine Project. It shows the design's surprisingly modern hydrodynamic hull form, with a single propeller aft, features that would be common in RN nuclear submarines a century later. Rudders were fitted above and below the propeller, with hydroplanes to port and starboard of it. These were used to incline the hull in order to dive or rise and to fine-tune depth control when running at periscope depth. The lack of fore-planes would have made depth control difficult in rough conditions. The tiny tower amidships was fitted with glass scuttles so that the boat could be conned from it while running trimmed-down on the surface, making her easier to control but a more difficult target for enemy gunners. Internal ballast tanks allowed a smooth hull form, with the flat-topped casing added to provide somewhere for the crew to stand when coming alongside in harbour. Just forward of the conning tower there was an attachment point for the coxswain to fix an external wheel for use when the boat was manoeuvring on the surface.

The very successful 'E' class formed the core of the Royal Navy's submarine force in the First World War and they continued to be built until 1917. These introduced watertight sub-division into the hull with two transverse bulkheads which divided the hull into three sections, although the boat could not remain afloat if either of the largest two compartments was completely flooded. The bulkheads also had the effect of strengthening the hull, which allowed the class to achieve a greater diving depth than previous boats. They displaced 662 tons on the surface and 807 tons dived. Their primary armament comprised three torpedo tubes, two of which were forward and one aft. Most mounted a 4-inch gun and some two, both of which were partially enclosed in the casing when dived to lessen underwater drag. Six boats were modified to carry up to twenty mines and several early boats were fitted with two broadside torpedo tubes, one firing to port and the other to starboard. Fifty-five 'E' class boats were built, two of which were for the RAN. Twenty-seven were lost on war service, including both of the Australian boats. Several 'E's achieved notable successes during the war, among them *AE 2* commanded by Lieutenant Commander H H G Stoker RN, which was the first boat to penetrate the Dardanelles during the

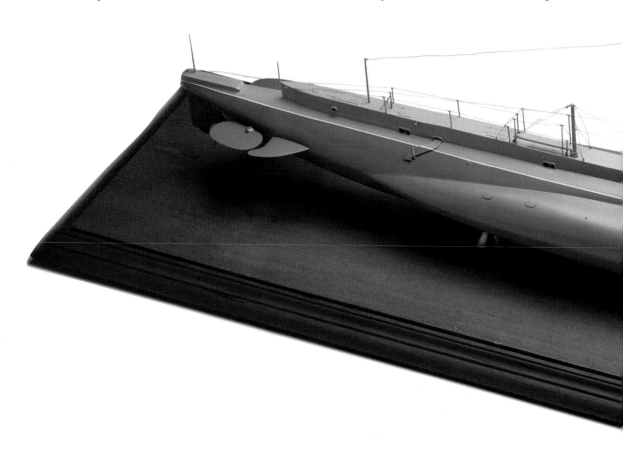

Gallipoli Campaign in 1915. She was subsequently lost on the Sea of Marmara. *E 11* also penetrated the Dardanelles, commanded by Lieutenant E H Nasmith RN, who was subsequently awarded the Victoria Cross for exploits which included sinking the Turkish pre-dreadnought battleship *Heirredin Barbarossa* and making a raft out of captured Turkish small craft that enabled his First Lieutenant to swim ashore with a number of demolition charges which he used to blow up a viaduct over which trains had been taking enemy troops to Gallipoli. In the North Sea as well, the 'E' class earned a high reputation.

This 1/48 scale model of HMAS *AE 2* from the Australian National Maritime Museum shows the exterior detail of an 'E' class submarine in considerable detail. Note especially the side or 'saddle' buoyancy tanks and the fore and aft hydroplanes with their fixed guards just forward of each of them. The models is fully rigged with W/T masts raised and its aerials rigged. Guardrails are fitted to the casing; these were only rigged in harbour and would have been removed and placed carefully in stowages within the casing while at sea. In the original design, the 'E' class had valves at the top and bottom of the saddle buoyancy tanks, both of which were opened to allow seawater in to reduce the boat's buoyancy. In practice the lower valves were left open, with seawater only kept out by air pressure within the tank so that boats could dive more quickly, since only the top valves needed to be opened to release the air. Once this practice was recognised and accepted, the lower valves were not even fitted and the holes in the bottom of the tank left open.

The 'E's were the first RN submarines to be fitted with accommodation capable of sustaining the ship's company on a protracted war patrol; arguably the most important addition being a toilet which could be flushed while the boat was submerged. This involved operating a complicated sequence of valves and levers with the penalty of 'getting your own back' if a mistake was made with the high-pressure air valve. The exact arrangement of valves differed between builders, increasing the risk of error for the unwary, but the same basic system remained in use until the 'A' class of 1945. (Australian National Maritime Museum)

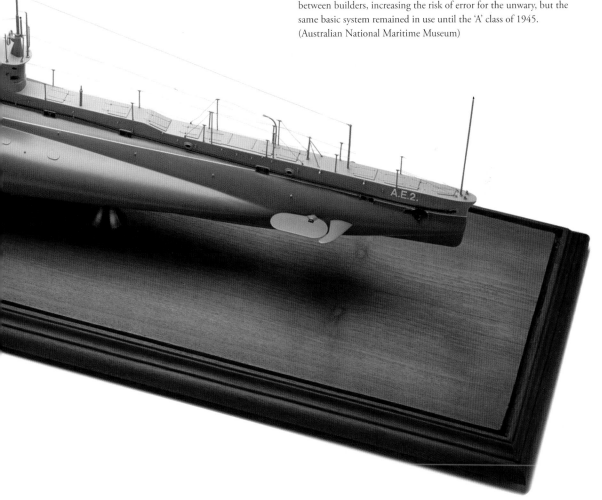

FEATURES OF A SUBMARINE

Unlike surface ships, submarines are able to control their buoyancy and sink below the surface, or dive, under control. They achieve this with large ballast tanks, a number of small trimming tanks and small moveable 'wings' fitted in pairs fore and aft known as hydroplanes. On the surface the ballast tanks are kept full of air, the boat weighs less than the water it displaces, and it floats. To dive, vents in the top of the tanks are opened allowing water to enter from other vents in the bottom which are kept constantly open to allow a rapid dive if necessary; the boat then weighs more than the water it displaces and it dives. By altering the amount of air and water in the ballast tanks a desired depth can be maintained, with fine tuning achieved by

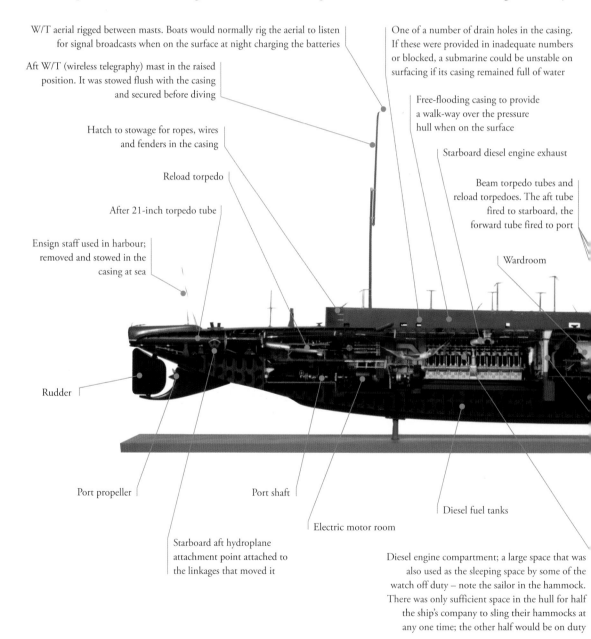

W/T aerial rigged between masts. Boats would normally rig the aerial to listen for signal broadcasts when on the surface at night charging the batteries

Aft W/T (wireless telegraphy) mast in the raised position. It was stowed flush with the casing and secured before diving

Hatch to stowage for ropes, wires and fenders in the casing

Reload torpedo

After 21-inch torpedo tube

Ensign staff used in harbour; removed and stowed in the casing at sea

Rudder

One of a number of drain holes in the casing. If these were provided in inadequate numbers or blocked, a submarine could be unstable on surfacing if its casing remained full of water

Free-flooding casing to provide a walk-way over the pressure hull when on the surface

Starboard diesel engine exhaust

Beam torpedo tubes and reload torpedoes. The aft tube fired to starboard, the forward tube fired to port

Wardroom

Port propeller

Port shaft

Diesel fuel tanks

Electric motor room

Starboard aft hydroplane attachment point attached to the linkages that moved it

Diesel engine compartment; a large space that was also used as the sleeping space by some of the watch off duty – note the sailor in the hammock. There was only sufficient space in the hull for half the ship's company to sling their hammocks at any one time; the other half would be on duty adjusting the water content in a number of small trimming tanks. With different salinity at differing depths, a static dive is difficult to attain, but as long the boat is moving forward, the hydroplanes can be used like the ailerons of an aeroplane to adjust and maintain depth. Ideally a boat would be trimmed to maintain neutral buoyancy at the depth at which it was operating and make minor adjustments with the hydroplanes. The rudder acts like that of any other vessel. Movement of people within the boat, the discharge of torpedoes and usage of fuel and stores, all cause changes in the boat's

centre of gravity which have to be adjusted for with the trimming tanks. To surface, the upper vents are closed and water is forced out of the bottom vents by compressed air stored in cylinders inside the hull. The 'E' class formed the backbone of the RN submarine force in the First World War and this model of *E 29* forms part of the Imperial War Museum's collection; it was made by her builder, Armstrong Whitworth, in 1921. At 1/24 scale the model is over 7 feet long, allowing a considerable amount of detail to be incorporated inside the cutaway sections. (Imperial War Museum MOD000098)

Search periscope in the raised position. The 'E' class was the first British submarine in which the lens of the search periscope could be rotated upwards to search for aircraft

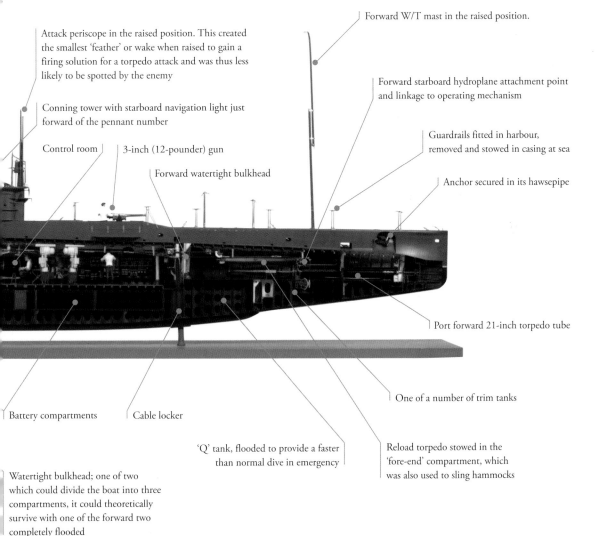

Forward W/T mast in the raised position.

Attack periscope in the raised position. This created the smallest 'feather' or wake when raised to gain a firing solution for a torpedo attack and was thus less likely to be spotted by the enemy

Forward starboard hydroplane attachment point and linkage to operating mechanism

Conning tower with starboard navigation light just forward of the pennant number

Guardrails fitted in harbour, removed and stowed in casing at sea

Control room   3-inch (12-pounder) gun

Anchor secured in its hawsepipe

Forward watertight bulkhead

Port forward 21-inch torpedo tube

One of a number of trim tanks

Battery compartments   Cable locker

'Q' tank, flooded to provide a faster than normal dive in emergency

Reload torpedo stowed in the 'fore-end' compartment, which was also used to sling hammocks

Watertight bulkhead; one of two which could divide the boat into three compartments, it could theoretically survive with one of the forward two completely flooded

FLEET SUBMARINES

Despite the success of the patrol submarine classes, Admiral Sir John Jellicoe believed that faster submarines had a role to play in close co-operation with surface fleets, and the Admiralty issued specifications for large submarines with a high surface speed capable of sailing in company with the battle fleet and then diving to intercept the enemy during a battle. There were obvious impracticalities with such a concept, not least the need for the submarine commanding officers to receive information from the battle fleet commander, to attempt to follow a long-range gunnery action between large numbers of ships through the lens of a periscope and to avoid being hit by those ships manoeuvring at high speed while they concentrated on the enemy surface fleet. Despite this, two designs were completed from 1916 onwards. The 'J' class had a dived displacement of 1820 tons and achieved 19.5 knots on the surface with three shafts, each driven by a 12-cylinder diesel engine. There were only two electric motors, one driving each of the wing shafts, giving an underwater speed of up to 10 knots for short periods. Seven 'J' class boats were completed but they proved to be too slow for operation with the fleet on the surface and too fast, big and expensive for use as patrol submarines. One was lost in the North Sea in 1918 and the others transferred to the RAN in 1919 but soon disposed of in post-war economies.

The next attempt produced the 'K' class, which were 339 feet long and had a dived displacement of

2566 tons, making them the largest submarines so far built, as well as the fastest, when the first was completed in 1916. Steam machinery of 10,500 horsepower on two shafts gave a surface speed of 24 knots but, for obvious reasons, the boiler fires had to be extinguished before the boats could dive. The original armament comprised: four bow and four beam 18-inch torpedo tubes, plus a twin rotating mount in the superstructure; two 4-inch low-angle and one 3-inch high-angle guns, the latter intended for use against aircraft while the boats operated on the surface.

The 'K' class were technically too advanced for their time, suffered a number of problems and were not popular in service. Given their great length, even a slight bow-down angle could put the bow below safe diving depth and accurate depth control was, therefore, of critical importance, but telemotor systems of immature design were used to operate the large number of trimming and diving tanks from the control room. Any fault could affect the trim and take the boat beyond the safe depth. However, the complex preparation for diving a 'K' boat was well thought through and usually took about five minutes but could be achieved in just under four. The oil-fired boilers had to be shut down and the funnels double-sealed then hinged down into the casing; but considerable heat was retained in the brickwork for a long period after diving, making the machinery spaces particularly unpleasant. Six 'K' class boats were lost in accidents during the war and another after the war.

This builder's model of a 'K' class submarine is in the collection of the Imperial War Museum and shows the boat with the original low freeboard. The search and attack periscopes are both shown raised and the W/T masts have been erected and rigged. The three guns can be seen forward of the conning tower, on top of the superstructure that housed the two funnels and on the after deck. The boat's two stubby funnels can be seen abaft the midships W/T mast. (Imperial War Museum MOD000099)

The original low bow was forced down when steaming at high speed into a rough, head sea and this problem had to be cured by fitting a large, flared forecastle structure known as a 'swan bow', and in many boats the deck gun forward of the conning tower was removed as it was unworkable in any but the calmest of conditions.

In the context of ambitious designs, mention should also be made of the 'M' class 'submarine monitors', two of which were completed in 1918 with single 12-inch Mark IX guns – taken from the spares held for the *Formidable* class pre-dreadnoughts – which could elevate to 20 degrees and train 15 degrees either side of the centreline. There were also four 18-inch torpedo tubes in the bow.

In a speech to the Institute of Naval Architects in 1920, Rear Admiral Dent, the Flag Officer Submarines, paid tribute to British submarine designers, highlighting the fact that during the war the British had built the largest submarines, the fastest submarines both on the surface and submerged, the submarines with the heaviest gun armament and the submarines with the heaviest torpedo armament.

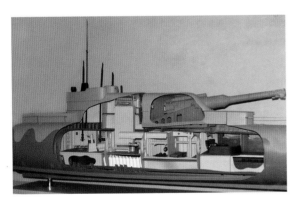

This cutaway model in the collection of the Science Museum shows the internal ammunition handling arrangements for the 12-inch gun and the control room under the conning tower of *M 1*. The attack periscope is in the raised position, the other masts are lowered. The gun was intended to be an alternative to torpedoes for engaging surface targets and in action the boat positioned itself with the gun muzzle about 6 feet clear of the sea surface about 1200 yards from the target. Firing was under periscope control and, at that range, a hit was almost certain. Exposure near the surface before firing was usually about 75 seconds but could be as little as 35; reloading could only be carried out on the surface and took about 3 minutes. Perhaps surprisingly, they proved to be a good design and were able to dive in only 90 seconds. *M 1* and *M 2* were completed to this design in 1918, while a third, *M 3*, was completed as a large minelayer. *M 1* was sunk in a collision off Start Point in 1925 and *M 2* was modified to carry a seaplane in its hangar in place of the gun in 1927. It foundered off Portland in 1932. (Photo by courtesy of Roger Branfill-Cook)

7: Other Warship Types

Throughout the First World War battleships remained the final arbiters of sea power, the ultimate strength behind the smaller warships and auxiliaries that carried out the everyday tasks of sea control. However, many of the most striking developments in the naval warfare of the period are best demonstrated by these less glamorous types, whose numbers, variety and technological improvement expanded at an unprecedented rate. The National Maritime Museum has a number of models in its collection that illustrate many of these ships and give an idea of their purpose and operation.

AIRCRAFT-CARRYING SHIPS

The first ship built specifically to operate seaplanes was the *Ark Royal*, completed in 1915, but the Royal Navy took up a number of merchant ships from trade to meet its expanded requirement for aircraft-carrying warships from 1914 onwards. At first it was assumed that seaplanes were the ideal aircraft since they could take-off from and land back onto the sea. Their support ships were thought of as 'floating hangars' without the need for flight decks, and the modified cruiser *Hermes* had operated as such in the 1913 fleet manoeuvres with canvas hangars fore and aft for two seaplanes, one of which was the first to have folding wings. *Ark Royal* followed the same idea but seaplanes were soon found to be a disappointment in operation because they were difficult to operate from open water and they lacked high performance in flight.

Numerous attempts were made by the Grand Fleet to launch air attacks from the sea. The first was an attempt on Christmas Day 1914 to attack Zeppelin

sheds believed to be at Cuxhaven by seaplanes from *Engadine, Riviera* and *Empress*. The raid was not a success but it did give an indication of what more capable aircraft operating from the decks of aircraft carriers could achieve in future. *Furious* launched a force of Sopwith Camel wheeled fighter-bombers from her flight deck in July 1918 which destroyed the German Zeppelins *L 54* and *L 60* in their sheds at Tondern, heralding a new era of naval air warfare. *Argus*, the world's first aircraft carrier capable of both launching and recovering aircraft on its flight deck, was completed in September 1918. After her initial trials, specially designed Sopwith T1 torpedo-bombers were embarked to prepare for an attack from her deck on the German High Seas Fleet in its harbours, the genesis of the idea from which the Japanese attack on Pearl Harbor evolved. The Armistice on 11 November 1918 came into effect just before the aircraft and their crews were declared to be ready but the tactics were demonstrated with outstanding effect by Sopwith T1s against the Royal Navy's Atlantic Fleet in Portland Harbour during manoeuvres held in 1919.

This well-detailed model of *Engadine* in 1/192 scale was made by Julian B Glossop and is in the collection of the Imperial War Museum. It shows the ship as she appeared after her full conversion in 1915. The large, box-shaped hangar structure is the most obvious feature, with a small deck space aft of it on which aircraft were prepared for flight before being lowered into the water by crane. Two cranes were fitted which folded flush with the after hangar bulkhead when not in use. The hangar had space for four Short Type 184 seaplanes stowed on trolleys which allowed aircraft to be moved on rails out to the working deck in rough weather. It was heated by steam radiators to keep the aircraft warm, and the workshops were equipped to repair wireless telegraphy sets, air weapons and engines, besides the facilities needed for carpenters' and fabric workers' repairs. There was a darkroom for processing reconnaissance photographs taken by aircraft and a powerful Marconi wireless set, used both to communicate with aircraft and to re-transmit their information with a stronger signal. She also had a fully functioning pigeon loft with the facilities needed to train birds to return to the ship when released from aircraft. Given the unreliable nature of wireless, it was hoped that these could bring back reconnaissance information or, in an emergency, news of when and where their aircraft had come down in the sea.

In 1916 she served with the battlecruisers and during the opening phase of the Battle of Jutland on 31 May 1916 Admiral Beatty ordered her to launch a seaplane to search for the German fleet. A Short Type 184 piloted by Flight Lieutenant Rutland RNAS with Paymaster Trewin RN as his observer was launched and located the enemy cruiser screen. Their wireless reports were taken in by *Engadine* and re-broadcast to the flagship *Lion* but, for whatever reason in the heat of battle, they were not acknowledged. This was the first time in history that an aircraft had taken part in a naval battle. This waterline model shows *Engadine* as she would have appeared at Jutland. She has one Short Type 184 folded on its trolley in the hangar, a second on the deck aft and a third in the water off the starboard side, waiting to be hoisted in by crane. She was lightly armed with four 12-pounder quick-firing high-angle guns distributed around the superstructure. In 1918 *Engadine* joined the Mediterranean Fleet and operated from Malta but she was sold back to her original owners after the end of hostilities. In 1933 she was re-sold for use as a ferry in the Philippines and renamed *Corregidor*. She hit a mine in Manilla Bay during the Japanese invasion in December 1941 and sank with heavy loss of life. (Imperial War Museum MOD000302)

This 1/700 model was made by Jim Baumann and shows *Furious* as she appeared in 1918 with the after 18-inch gun turret removed and replaced by a landing deck with a hangar beneath it. This reconstruction followed the world's first carrier landing on the 228-foot take-off deck by Squadron Commander E H Dunning DSC RNAS on 2 August 1917. He was killed five days later attempting a further landing on the deck but he had demonstrated that deck landing was possible and subsequent aircraft carrier development stemmed from his outstanding example. *Furious'* pilots believed that turbulence aft of the central bridge structure and funnel would make landing on the after deck dangerous and experience was to prove them right. Despite the after deck's failure for routine landings, the second hangar doubled the size of the air group that could be embarked and *Furious* took part in some of the first naval air battles in history during 1918. The model contains a wealth of detail and shows windbreaks raised to protect the aircraft on the forward deck; the forward lift is down and folded aircraft are visible struck down in both the forward and aft hangars. The non-rigid airship *SSZ 59* is portrayed landing on the after deck in the summer of 1918 during trials to evaluate the feasibility of refuelling airships on a carrier deck to extend their radius of action. The handling party is particularly well portrayed and helps to give an excellent idea of one of naval aviation's iconic early activities. (By courtesy of Jim Baumann)

ANTI-SUBMARINE ESCORTS

A requirement was identified soon after the outbreak of war in 1914 for a small, cheap, destroyer-type vessel which could be built quickly for anti-submarine escort duties. The resulting design was identified as the 'P' class and individual ships were given numbers beginning with *P 11* rather than names. Twenty-four were ordered in 1915 and more followed in 1916 and 1917. They were built of mild steel rather than the high-tensile steel of major warships to save time and cost since rivet holes could be punched rather than drilled. They had a low silhouette (freeboard was just over 6 feet amidships) designed to look like a surfaced submarine, and a draught of only 8 feet which was intended to make them difficult to torpedo. Armament comprised a single 4-inch gun on a 'bandstand' forward of the bridge, a pom-pom aft and two single, trainable 14-inch torpedo tubes. They displaced 600 tons and twin-shaft machinery of 4000 horsepower gave a speed of 22 knots. The single large rudder gave an impressively tight turning circle and they proved to be well-liked, if somewhat wet, ships with a ship's company of only 55. Many were built by yards unused to warship construction and they took anything from nine to eighteen months to build. Most were contracted on a cost-plus-profit basis and the average cost to the Admiralty was £104,000. Later derivatives were given the appearance of small merchant ships to act as Q-ships (see below) and designated as PC-boats although retaining the same machinery and armament. Some P-boats remained in service after 1918, the last being scrapped in 1939.

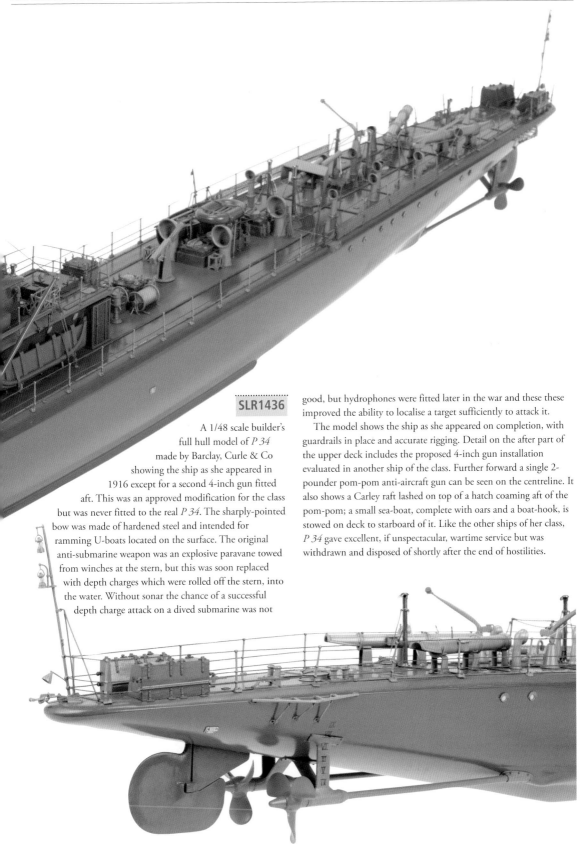

SLR1436

A 1/48 scale builder's full hull model of *P 34* made by Barclay, Curle & Co showing the ship as she appeared in 1916 except for a second 4-inch gun fitted aft. This was an approved modification for the class but was never fitted to the real *P 34*. The sharply-pointed bow was made of hardened steel and intended for ramming U-boats located on the surface. The original anti-submarine weapon was an explosive paravane towed from winches at the stern, but this was soon replaced with depth charges which were rolled off the stern, into the water. Without sonar the chance of a successful depth charge attack on a dived submarine was not good, but hydrophones were fitted later in the war and these these improved the ability to localise a target sufficiently to attack it.

The model shows the ship as she appeared on completion, with guardrails in place and accurate rigging. Detail on the after part of the upper deck includes the proposed 4-inch gun installation evaluated in another ship of the class. Further forward a single 2-pounder pom-pom anti-aircraft gun can be seen on the centreline. It also shows a Carley raft lashed on top of a hatch coaming aft of the pom-pom; a small sea-boat, complete with oars and a boat-hook, is stowed on deck to starboard of it. Like the other ships of her class, *P 34* gave excellent, if unspectacular, wartime service but was withdrawn and disposed of shortly after the end of hostilities.

UNCONVENTIONAL RESPON

The absence of a reliable method of locating submarines in the early part of the war led to some ingenious – and sometimes rather desperate – methods of countering the threat from U-boats to Allied merchant shipping. One such was the Q-ship, a decoy usually converted from a merchantman, although a few ex-naval vessels also served in the role; armed with hidden quick-firing guns and torpedoes, they were disguised to look like a harmless small merchant ship. The concept was to induce the U-boat to surface in order to use its gun on what appeared to be a target too small to warrant a torpedo. When the enemy was on the surface, guns would be uncovered and fire opened before it had a chance to dive. Q-ships were manned by volunteers and often used 'false crews' who made a show of abandoning ship to deceive the enemy into thinking that their target was an empty 'sitting duck'. About a dozen U-boats were sunk by Q-ships – a relatively small return for the large numbers of decoy ships deployed.

Part of the Imperial War Museum collection, this full-hull model depicts *Hyderabad*, which was the only purpose-built Q-ship, constructed in only four months and completed in August 1917. She had a remarkably shallow draught of only 3 feet 8 inches, seen clearly on the model, so that torpedoes would hopefully pass harmlessly under her keel. This model depicts some of the concealed armament: a 4-inch gun in a deckhouse abaft the funnel; a 12-pounder on the poop (usually hidden under a collapsing deckhouse); two of the four bomb-throwers (under the false hatches fore and aft); and the portside pair of torpedo launching cradles (in the hull under the bridge). There is another 12-pounder on a 'disappearing' mounting under the forecastle and there was also a pair of depth charge throwers. The gun right aft would have been left on show since by this stage of the war DAMS (defensively armed merchant ships) usually carried at least one gun on the poop. The holds were filled with barrels and materials such as cork or wood so that even if hit by the enemy she would remain afloat. (Imperial War Museum MOD000270)

THE U-BOAT MENACE

Escort vessels and Q-ships required U-boats to come to them in order to bring them to action, but by 1918 large minefields laid at depth and just below the surface in the English Channel and North Sea limited the options for enemy passage to their targets west of the United Kingdom. However, coastal U-boats and torpedo craft continued to operate out of the occupied Belgian ports, posing a significant threat in the English Channel. In April 1918 a radical method of limiting U-boat activities was attempted, with a naval force intending to sink blockships in the canal at Zeebrugge to prevent U-boats and destroyers getting to sea from the inland port of Bruges. A similar attack on Ostend took place several weeks later. Obsolete cruisers were used as blockships and the cruiser *Vindictive*, together with several modified ferries, were used to carry the assault force that seized the mole with the aim of suppressing enemy fire while the blocking operation took place. The operation was only a partial success since the canal was not completely blocked, but during the gallant action on the early morning of 23 April 1918 eleven men won the VC, a further twenty-one the DSO and twenty-nine the DSC.

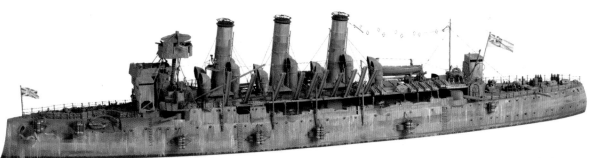

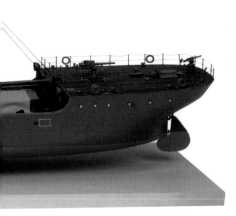

Vindictive was an *Arrogant* class protected cruiser, built by Chatham Dockyard and completed in 1900, with an armament in 1914 of ten 6-inch guns and three 18-inch torpedo tubes. She had a 3-inch armoured deck. She was already considered obsolescent by 1914 and was in use as a tender to the Torpedo School, *Vernon*, at Portsmouth. On the outbreak of war, however, she was brought forward for active service in the 9th Cruiser Squadron patrolling the mid-Atlantic. From 1915 she served on the South Atlantic Station and later in the White Sea during 1916-17 before being fitted out as an assault ship in 1918.

This model was made by Norman Ough and shows *Vindictive* in his usual meticulous detail as she appeared on 23 April 1918 when she was used to run alongside the Zeebrugge mole with storming parties of sailors and Royal Marines. The ship was considerably modified for the purpose and new equipment included an 11-inch howitzer, two 7.5-inch howitzers, two flame-throwers, two 'pom-poms' and six Lewis machine-guns in the foretop, besides retaining some of her original armament. She was fitted extensively with splinter mats and had a false, flush deck built from the forecastle to the quarterdeck on the port side, which was to be against the mole. From this, fourteen narrow gangways were fitted, visible on the port side of the model, over which the storming parties disembarked under fire. After Zeebrugge, by then famous if somewhat battered, she was expended as a blockship in the attack on the Ostend Canal that was carried out on 10 May 1918. Her wreck was subsequently raised and scrapped in 1920. (Imperial War Museum MOD000352-1)

MINESWEEPERS

The Royal Navy was aware of the potential threat from mines before 1914 and in 1911 a special section of the RNR had been organised to operate trawlers requisitioned for use as minesweepers. In September 1914 the Admiralty gave instructions for the construction of a large number of ships to be capable of minesweeping, anti-submarine work and target-towing under the Emergency War Programme. The resulting ships evolved as the 'Flower' class sloops, built in three distinct groups with further ships based on this design built as Q-ships. They were constructed to merchant ship standards so that they could be built in yards unused to naval work but this increased both their size and cost. With slight differences between batches they were 267 feet long with an armament of two single 4.7-inch or 4-inch guns and a number of smaller weapons. Features intended to help them survive a mine detonation included a triple bottom forward, a magazine above water level and coal bunkers that could be made watertight to provide a reserve of buoyancy. Despite this, the Royal Navy lost 9 out of the 72 ships in the class. The masts were designed to carry a sailing rig, intended to help keep the vessel steady at slow speed.

SLR0113 A 1/48 scale builder's full-hull model showing *Snapdragon*, one of the ships of the third batch of the 'Flower' class, as she appeared in 1916. The quarterdeck has the full outfit of minesweeping and towing winches. The un-shielded 4.7-inch guns can be seen on the forecastle and in a superfiring position above the quarterdeck with several smaller guns mounted in the area aft of the two funnels. The boats are superbly finished and other details include a chart on the chart table on the bridge and a quantity of rope inside an open locker on deck. Accommodation ladders are rigged on the port and starboard sides aft.

Snapdragon was built by Ropner's Yard at Stockton-on-Tees, launched on 21 December 1915 and commissioned two months later. She served in the Mediterranean as an escort vessel and rescued the crew of a British collier that had been sunk by a U-boat; whilst stopped in the water the U-boat fired two torpedoes at her but both missed. In 1918 she joined other escorts in engaging and sinking a U-boat that was sighted on the surface, subsequently picking up thirty-three survivors. It was *UB 68* and her commanding officer, Lieutenant Karl Dönitz (later to mastermind the Second world War U-boat campaign), spent the remainder of the war in a British prisoner of war camp. *Snapdragon* paid off in 1919 but was re-commissioned in 1920 for use as a target-towing vessel for fleet gunnery practice. She was finally discarded in 1934 but several of her sister-ships survived to see service in the Second World War.

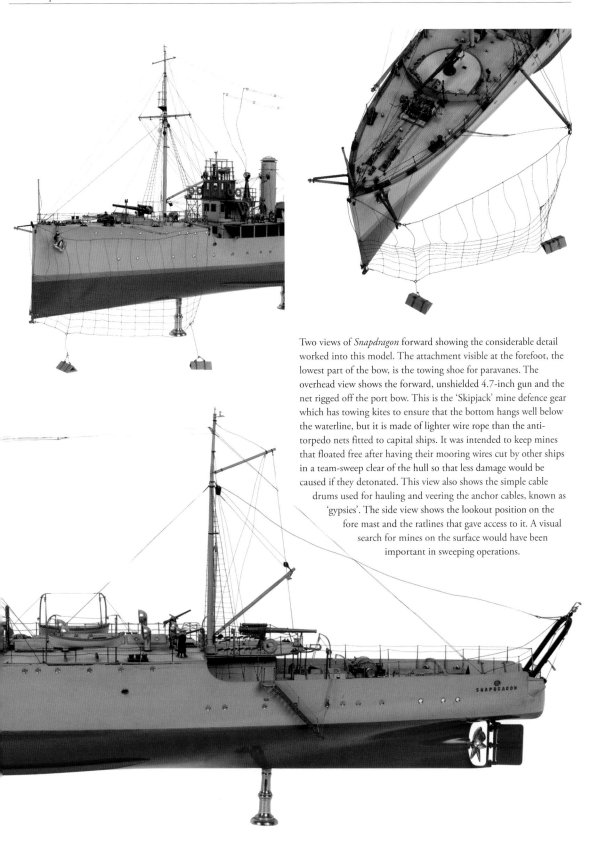

Two views of *Snapdragon* forward showing the considerable detail
worked into this model. The attachment visible at the forefoot, the
lowest part of the bow, is the towing shoe for paravanes. The
overhead view shows the forward, unshielded 4.7-inch gun and the
net rigged off the port bow. This is the 'Skipjack' mine defence gear
which has towing kites to ensure that the bottom hangs well below
the waterline, but it is made of lighter wire rope than the anti-
torpedo nets fitted to capital ships. It was intended to keep mines
that floated free after having their mooring wires cut by other ships
in a team-sweep clear of the hull so that less damage would be
caused if they detonated. This view also shows the simple cable
drums used for hauling and veering the anchor cables, known as
'gypsies'. The side view shows the lookout position on the
fore mast and the ratlines that gave access to it. A visual
search for mines on the surface would have been
important in sweeping operations.

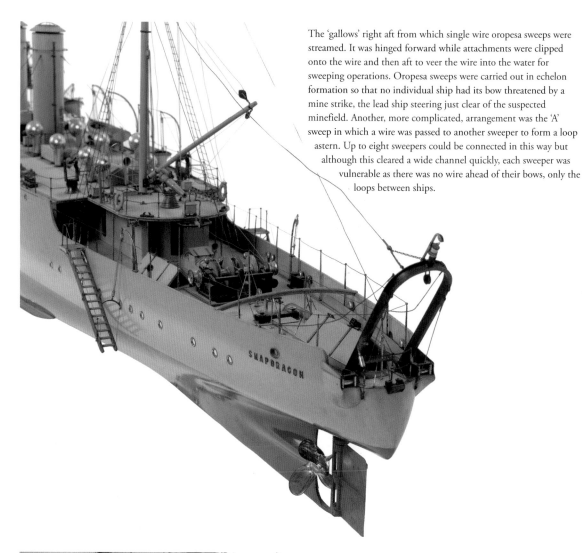

The 'gallows' right aft from which single wire oropesa sweeps were streamed. It was hinged forward while attachments were clipped onto the wire and then aft to veer the wire into the water for sweeping operations. Oropesa sweeps were carried out in echelon formation so that no individual ship had its bow threatened by a mine strike, the lead ship steering just clear of the suspected minefield. Another, more complicated, arrangement was the 'A' sweep in which a wire was passed to another sweeper to form a loop astern. Up to eight sweepers could be connected in this way but although this cleared a wide channel quickly, each sweeper was vulnerable as there was no wire ahead of their bows, only the loops between ships.

An overhead view of the sweep deck aft showing the powerful winch from which the sweep wires were paid out and recovered. The two objects that look like small tents are the towing kites that set the depth of the oropesa sweep wire. It was lowered on a kite wire to the required depth and the sweep wire, veered on a separate winch, passed through a snatch block on top of it. It was, in turn, pulled clear of the ship's centreline by an otter board suspended beneath a float to maintain the sweep depth. Wires were taken from the winch, over the bar across the deck that prevented them from snagging fittings on the deck, through the pulley on the 'gallows' and into the water. The float, otter board, cutters and the kite had to be attached to their pendants in the correct order after the wire had passed through their pulleys on being veered, and removed in reverse order as it was hauled in. The deck was a dangerous place during sweeping operations and extreme caution was needed when working on it. The single propeller and simple rudder can be seen in this full-hull model and both accommodation ladders are rigged in their working positions. The attachment on top of the 'gallows' is a light fitting to help deploy sweeps in the dark.

Midships details of *Snapdragon* showing the fore mast, bridge, wheelhouse and funnels. Like most vessels of the era, the bridge and wheelhouse were constructed of wood to minimise interference with the magnetic compasses, although in service they were painted grey. The open bridge has a compass binnacle, chart table and a mechanical semaphore arm. Below it is the wheelhouse and chartroom. The bridge wings and the decks beneath were used by marksmen with rifles who shot and detonated mines that had floated to the surface after being cut from their moorings, usually spotted by the lookout first; at night they were assisted by the two 20-inch searchlights. There are two steam sirens on the fore funnel. Minesweepers operated in groups on a line of bearing when using both types of sweep and the high, open bridge gave the commanding officer the best view of the other ships. Semaphore gave a quick and secure method of inter-ship communications but there was also a yardarm for signal flag groups, wireless telegraphy and the searchlights were capable of sending messages in morse code.

PADDLE MINESWEEPERS

By May 1915 experience with requisitioned vessels led the Admiralty to recognise the usefulness of paddle minesweepers in shallow water, and twenty-four ships of the *Ascot* class were ordered for delivery in 1916, followed by a further eight ships to an improved design in 1918. All named after racecourses, the *Ascot* class had a length of 245 feet and a beam of 58 feet across the paddles. Considerable care was taken with the hull's sub-division and the boiler rooms were situated fore and aft of the engine room, thus the two funnels were a considerable distance apart. There were eleven watertight compartments and the hull was strengthened to withstand the shock of a mine detonating close by. The watertight bulkheads were not penetrated by doors and fore and aft access past them had to be by climbing up to the upper deck through vertical hatches and then down again on the other side. The class displaced 800 tons and the 1600 horsepower engine gave a maximum speed of about 15 knots. They were also designed to carry two Sopwith Baby seaplane fighters for use against Zeppelins but, despite the success of trials in two of the ships, none were embarked for routine operations. One of the drawbacks with paddle propulsion was that thrust varied with the depth of the paddles and even a slight list made it difficult to hold a steady course. Since it was essential that swept channels through minefields followed an accurate, straight course, the *Ascot*s had tanks capable of holding up to ten tons of water fitted in both paddle sponsons. With one side full and the other empty they could correct a list of up to 5 degrees. Two 12-pounder guns were fitted, one forward and one aft, and the ship's company amounted to 52 men.

SLR1438 A 1/48 scale full-hull builder's model depicting *Ludlow*. It was made in collaboration between the Goole Shipbuilding Company and the Dundee Shipbuilding Company. *Ludlow* was built in the Goole yard and despite the utilitarian role of these ships, the model's minesweeping gear and the rigging are extremely well constructed; many of the fittings are finished in gunmetal using a process that involved the use of arsenic. Only a month after her completion, on 1 May 1916 near the Shipwash in Suffolk, *Ludlow* detonated a mine which blew off her stern. Five men were killed and seven injured. Initially she stayed afloat long enough to be taken in tow by *Pontefract* but her engine room bulkhead had been damaged and she gradually flooded and eventually sank before reaching safety. Another minesweeper in her squadron, *Totnes*, also hit a mine but her ship's company managed to keep her afloat. Other vessels in the squadron, which included *Gatwick*, *Cheltenham* and *Doncaster*, found and destroyed 53 German mines in five months. Other than *Ludlow*, four further ships of the class were lost on war service.

SLR2109 Although it does not show the machinery fitted to *Ludlow*, this 1/36 scale model gives a good idea of similar paddle-wheel engine design. It was made by the manufacturers John Penn and Son in 1883 and depicts the machinery fitted in the composite sloop HMS *Sphinx*. Note the 'feathering' paddle wheels, whose gearing was designed to give each paddle-board the most efficient passage through the water.

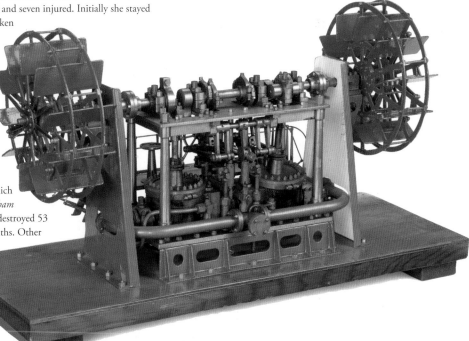

Coastal motor boats (CMBs)

The 55-foot coastal motor boats designed by Thornycroft were among the most exciting new warship types developed after 1914. They evolved from a 1915 proposal by officers in the Harwich Force that small, high-speed torpedo boats could be carried by a mother-ship to the German coast and used to attack the High Seas Fleet in its harbours. Cheap, expendable and able to skim over minefields because their draught could be measured in inches when the hull was planing at high speed, there was merit in the proposal, and twelve boats were built and operated by the Dover Patrol from 1916. It had, originally, been intended that these boats would be light enough, with their 18-inch torpedoes in place, to be hoisted onto larger warships by the davits used to hoist a 30-foot motor boat and weight was, therefore, a critical factor. This meant that a conventional torpedo tube could not be fitted and it was eventually decided to push the torpedo out over the stern, tail first. The boats had a speed about equal to that of the torpedo and it was calculated that they could quickly turn out of its way as it began to run. Trials at the torpedo school proved that the scheme actually worked and this launch method was adopted for all coastal motor boats. The early boats were 40 feet long and had a 250 brake horsepower motor which gave a speed of up to 34 knots. Forty-four were ordered from several builders but seventeen were cancelled at the end of the war.

Thornycroft anticipated that a larger version would be required and designed the 55-foot coastal motor boat in 1916. Orders followed in 1917 for large numbers to be built by Thornycroft and several sub-contractors with a variety of different engines ranging from 750 to 900

horsepower; all of them exceeded 30 knots and many reached 40 knots under ideal conditions. The 55-foot boats were capable of carrying two torpedoes but most were only fitted with one. Others were modified to carry two or four depth charges in addition to a single torpedo. Two or four Lewis guns were mounted on pillars to give wide arcs of fire at both low and high angles. They were not given names but were identified with the letters CMB followed by an individual number.

This full-hull model shows a 'standard' Thornycroft 55-foot coastal motor boat rather than an individual vessel. It was made by John Thornycroft & Co and depicts a boat on its launching trolley, appearing much as a real vessel would have done except for the gold-plated detailing. The sharply-stepped chine hull construction which gave the vessels their exceptionally high speed was based on pre-war racing hydroplanes; its form can be seen clearly amidships as can the two shafts and their propellers. The gold plating does have the effect of making the details stand out and this makes the two rudders quite conspicuous, together with the twin Lewis machine-guns mounted on the port side of the cockpit. The engines were mounted in the deeper part of the hull forward of the cockpit and an air intake for them can be seen just ahead of the forward mast. A normal crew comprised a commanding officer, coxswain, stoker/mechanic and one or two gunners. Two rails, each 5 feet long, can be seen above the rudders. These formed the after part of the trough in which the torpedo was carried and ensured that, when it dropped into the water, the weapon's contact detonator would fall clear of the motor boat's transom stern. By 1917 wireless transmitters and receivers had reduced in weight and bulk to the extent that they could be fitted in small warships, and the two raked masts were fitted to carry the necessary aerial array. In action the boat

would aim straight at its target and approach it at maximum speed, the securing straps that held the torpedo in place having been released. Just short of 1000 yards from the target the torpedo was released and as it began to run towards the target the boat would veer sharply to one side, leaving it to run. The model shows four depth charges stowed, two on either side, aft of the cockpit. These could be dropped on a U-boat over a position where it had been seen to dive. Alternatively they could be dropped close alongside an enemy ship to cause underwater damage when they detonated. The motor boat's high speed would have carried it clear before their detonation. The Lewis guns on the cockpit could be used either to suppress enemy fire during the run to the target or, more likely, against aircraft, since the boats operated by the Dover Patrol were frequently attacked by enemy seaplanes. Made of wood and full of petrol, these boats were vulnerable to enemy fire. The metal device on the front of the cockpit was a torpedo sight, used to calculate the deflection needed to launch the torpedo against a moving target. These boats gave good service operating out of Dover and off the east coast of the UK, but their greatest exploits took place in the Baltic in 1919 during operations against the Bolsheviks. A large force of boats attacked an enemy fleet in Kronstadt and sank the battleships *Petropavlosk* and *Andrei Pervosvanni*, together with a submarine depot ship, in a textbook attack.

A close-in detail of the model's stern showing the rails over which the torpedo was launched. Its contra-rotating propellers can be seen just above, but clear of, the transom stern. Note the linked rudders and their close proximity to the two propellers, designed to give good manoeuvrability at both high and low speeds. This view also shows the curved stowages from which the depth charges could be rolled by hand.

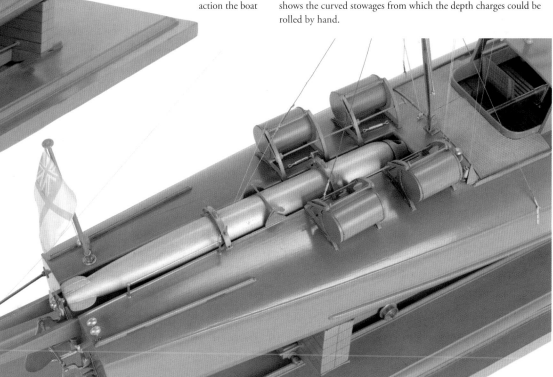

BOATS AND BOAT STOWAGE

During the First World War the majority of large, operational warships were not secured alongside when in port but anchored out in sheltered harbours such as Scapa Flow, Cromarty Firth, the Firth of Forth and other bases. Boats were, therefore, a vital part of their equipment to ferry officers and liberty men ashore and back again, and to collect mail, stores, chart amendments and the large number of small items needed to keep the fleet informed and effective. They came in a variety of different shapes and sizes but all had to be seaworthy enough to cope with the conditions in large anchorages that were often swept by storms. In long periods of waiting, the smaller boats were often the only immediate form of recreation available. At sea they had to be stowed clear of gun blast to avoid damage, especially in capital ships. Some were used as sea-boats and were lowered from davits.

Larger boats were mainly used in harbour and were lifted from their stowages by derricks attached to masts or king-posts for the purpose, and this had a significant effect on the layout of major warships. Some of the larger steam pinnaces and picket boats could be armed with small quick-firing guns and lightweight torpedoes for offensive use in inshore operations. All boats had an important use in landing parties of 'bluejackets', marines or military forces in amphibious operations, and many of the troops landed in the assault waves at Gallipoli were landed by ships' boats from the larger warships, the oared boats towed by the steam-powered ones in long lines. Large ships' boats were commanded by midshipmen, often giving them their first experience of ship-handling, the leadership of a small groups of men and, at Gallipoli, combat.

The builder's model of *Indomitable* demonstrates the principal boat stowage on a battlecruiser. Stowed on forward superstructure as clear as possible from the blast of the midships 12-inch guns is a mixture of oared cutters, whalers and gigs. They were lowered into the water and recovered by the derrick stowed in the foreground, which is attached to the king-post alongside the after (left-hand) funnel. The derrick falls could be worked by hand or by the steam winch visible under the stern of the nearest cutter. A similar derrick was sited to port.

Steam picket boats, cutters and a whaler were stowed on *Indomitable*'s after superstructure. The two forward cutters to port and starboard are sea-boats on quadrantal davits, secured by gripes. The remaining boats are stowed on chocks and more usually used in harbour. They were worked by the derrick attached to the main mast. Note the steam boats' folded funnels. The official outfit of boats for this ship was: two 50-foot steam pinnaces, a 36-foot sailing pinnace, a 32-foot sailing launch, two 32-foot life cutters, one 32-foot cutter, one 30-foot gig, three 27-foot whalers, one 16-foot dinghy and a 13½-foot balsa raft. (By courtesy of Ian Johnston)

Detail of HMAS *Australia*'s after superstructure boat stowage. The boats include steam pinnaces and cutters worked by the derrick attached to the main mast. The two cutters rigged as sea-boats and turned out to port and starboard are particularly interesting as their quadrantal davits are hinged on the superstructure roof to avoid blast from 'P' and 'Q' turrets when they fired on an aft bearing with the boats in the stowed position at sea. This made them very high above the deck and a long climb for sailors to man them. (Australian War Memorial)

A 30-foot cutter rigged as a sea-boat complete with oars turned out on radial davits on *Barham*'s starboard side amidships. They are not yet ready for lowering as the crossed gripes are still holding them firmly against the griping spar with its padded 'puddings', keeping them secure despite the ship's movement. (By courtesy of Ian Johnston)

A steam pinnace from HMAS *Australia* armed with a 3-pounder quick-firing gun forward. It could also be armed with two 14-inch torpedoes for inshore operations. When disarmed, pinnaces were frequently used as admiral's barges and this model carries a vice-admiral's flag on the bow. (Australian National Maritime Museum)

SLR1501 Model of a 27-foot Montagu whaler presented to R H Curran, coxswain of the boat that won the 1931 RNVR inter-port whaler race. It shows the mast bracket on the second thwart from forward and the keel box amidships. Under oars the boat's crew comprised five oarsmen and a coxswain. Whalers of this type remained in service until the 1960s when they were replaced by a motorised derivative capable of sail, oar or mechanical propulsion.

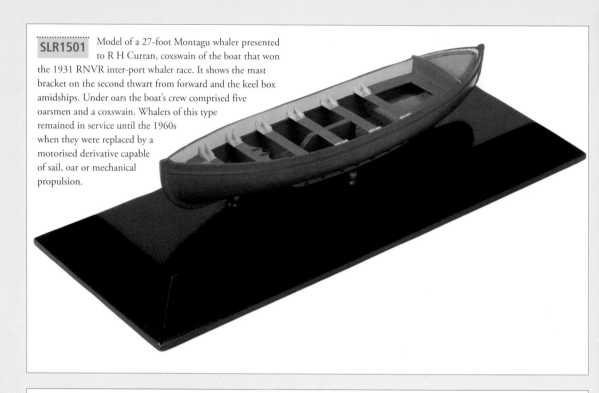

SLR0015 The model shows the extensive outfit of boats in the scout cruiser *Forward*. The forward two to port and starboard are 30-foot oared cutters rigged as sea-boats in quadrantal davits. Aft of them to port and starboard are 25-foot whalers suspended from radial davits. On the port side aft there is a 30-foot steam cutter in radial davits and on the starboard side there is a 38-foot oared cutter or 'troop boat', also in radial davits.

SLR0114 Midships detail of the TBD *Boyne* showing two Berthon folding boats stowed on either side of the fore funnel. After assembly they were lowered into the water by the derrick seen in its stowed position on the mast. Of interest, a similar folding boat was to have been carried by HM Rigid Airship Number 1, unofficially known as 'Mayfly', had it not been lost by accident in 1911.

SLR1436A Carley raft stowed forward of the 2-pounder 'pom-pom' in the anti-submarine patrol vessel *P 34*, inboard of a 13½-foot gig. Carley rafts gave positive buoyancy for groups of survivors and were often equipped with paddles and ration boxes, but they offered no protection against the cold and many sailors who reached them after a sinking soon died of hypothermia. Their buoyancy was often reduced by over-zealous painting in order to look smart on the upper deck. Despite this, they remained in use until the 1950s.

RIVER GUNBOATS

During the nineteenth century the Royal Navy had gained considerable experience of riverine warfare and developed a type of shallow-draught gunboat specifically for the purpose. A standing flotilla of these was stationed on Chinese rivers, so when war broke out and similar vessels were ordered for employment in other theatres, describing them whilst under construction as 'China gunboats' was a convincing strategic disguise. There were two main classes of these, the smaller 'Fly' class being designed for use on the Tigris in support of the Mesopotamia campaign, and a larger class, named after insects, originally intended to oppose the flotilla of powerful river monitors the Austro-Hungarians operated on the Danube. However, before the 'Insect' class could be completed the Serbian front collapsed and they were diverted to other theatres in Egypt, the Persian Gulf and Mesopotamia, and even to UK East Coast ports for anti-Zeppelin duties. All but one of them did eventually serve on the China Station after 1918. They displaced 645 tons but could float in only 4 feet of water with the two shafts contained in tunnels. Reciprocating steam machinery of 2000 horsepower gave a top speed in the region of 14 knots and the three rudders gave exceptionally good manoeuvrability at low speed. Armament comprised two 6-inch and two 12-pounder guns plus numerous smaller quick-firing weapons.

SLR0091 *Sandpiper* portrayed in a 1/32 scale model made by Yarrow of Poplar, her builder, is a good example of a pre-war China gunboat. It is a waterline model mounted on a glass sea base, with a single mast and has a fighting-top fitted with a Maxim machine-gun. An awning is rigged over the central superstructure and the model shows the vessel as she appeared in service with the wooden deck looking particularly realistic. She was 108 feet long, had a displacement of 85 tons and her twin-shaft, triple-expansion steam machinery gave a speed of about 9 knots. She had a draught of only 2 feet and the three rudders were mounted on the square vertical transom stern since there was no room for them under the ship's bottom. Armament comprised two single 6-pounder guns and a number of Maxim machine-guns mounted on the bridge deck under the awning. The superstructure has both scuttles and firing slits for rifles and contained accommodation for the ship's company. The shallow draught would have made a sea passage to the Far East dangerous and so, after her initial completion in 1883, *Sandpiper* was dismantled and shipped to Hong Kong Dockyard where she was re-erected. Together with her sister-ships *Snipe, Robin* and *Nightingale* she spent her entire operational career on the China Station and was sold off locally for scrap after 1918.

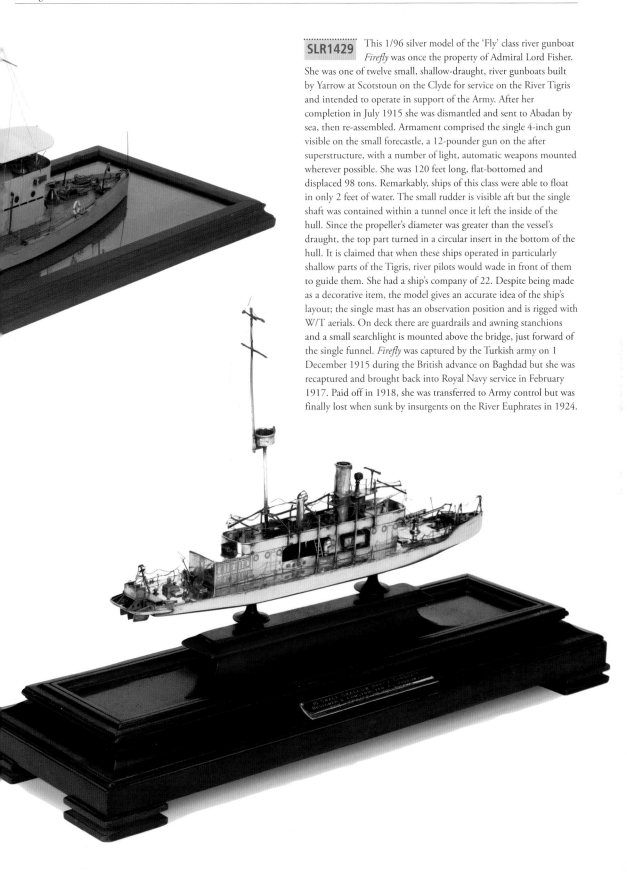

SLR1429 This 1/96 silver model of the 'Fly' class river gunboat *Firefly* was once the property of Admiral Lord Fisher. She was one of twelve small, shallow-draught, river gunboats built by Yarrow at Scotstoun on the Clyde for service on the River Tigris and intended to operate in support of the Army. After her completion in July 1915 she was dismantled and sent to Abadan by sea, then re-assembled. Armament comprised the single 4-inch gun visible on the small forecastle, a 12-pounder gun on the after superstructure, with a number of light, automatic weapons mounted wherever possible. She was 120 feet long, flat-bottomed and displaced 98 tons. Remarkably, ships of this class were able to float in only 2 feet of water. The small rudder is visible aft but the single shaft was contained within a tunnel once it left the inside of the hull. Since the propeller's diameter was greater than the vessel's draught, the top part turned in a circular insert in the bottom of the hull. It is claimed that when these ships operated in particularly shallow parts of the Tigris, river pilots would wade in front of them to guide them. She had a ship's company of 22. Despite being made as a decorative item, the model gives an accurate idea of the ship's layout; the single mast has an observation position and is rigged with W/T aerials. On deck there are guardrails and awning stanchions and a small searchlight is mounted above the bridge, just forward of the single funnel. *Firefly* was captured by the Turkish army on 1 December 1915 during the British advance on Baghdad but she was recaptured and brought back into Royal Navy service in February 1917. Paid off in 1918, she was transferred to Army control but was finally lost when sunk by insurgents on the River Euphrates in 1924.

SLR1431 A model of *Tarantula*, one of the twelve large 'Insect' class, made to the standard 1/48 scale for her builder, Wood, Skinner & Company of Newcastle upon Tyne in 1915 when she was completed. The model was intended to appear striking rather than realistic and has dark grey upper works on a dark grey and black hull with gold-plated details, but for most of its life the real ship would actually have been painted white. While not accurate, the gold detailing does stand out well and the 6-inch guns fore and aft of the superstructure can be seen clearly; neither had a gun shield to protect the crew in action. The 12-pounders are mounted on the superstructure in superfiring positions, the forward one sharing space with the spartan bridge structure. Two Hotchkiss quick-firing 3-pounders are mounted on top of the superstructure aft of the single funnel.

Tarantula was one of four of the class towed to the Persian Gulf in 1916 to form part of the British offensive that eventually captured Baghdad. After the war she was towed to the Far East and served on the China Station until 1940 when she was moved to Trincomalee for use as a store ship and as office space for senior officers' staffs. Finally on 1 May 1946 she was towed to sea and sunk as a target by the destroyers *Carron* and *Carysfort*.

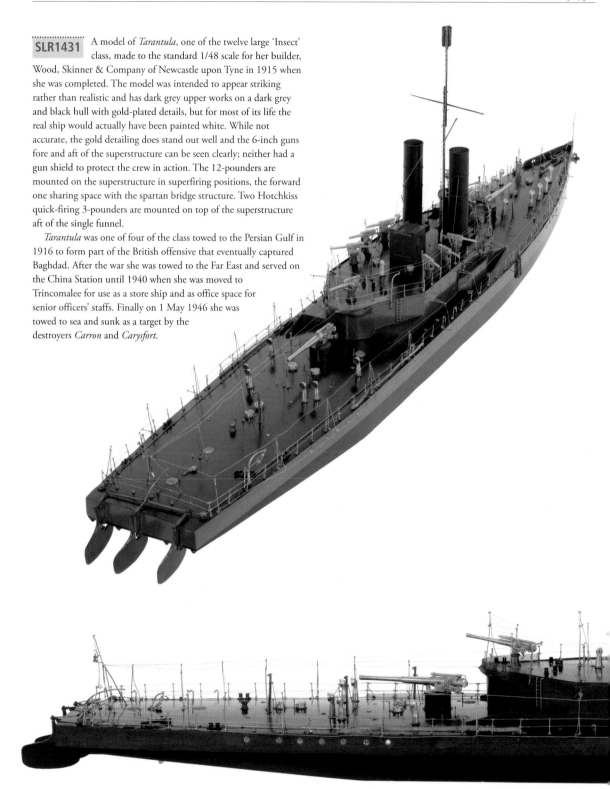

The tunnel arrangement that protected the shafts and propellers from damage if the vessel grounded and the three rudders positioned right at the stern. The model is fitted onto a bevelled, mirrored base to show this unusual shaft arrangement when viewed from above.

8: Merchantmen at War

ARMED MERCHANT CRUISERS

Some preparations were made before 1914 to fit guns to liners selected for use as armed merchant cruisers (AMCs). By late August 1914 thirteen liners had been fitted out and by the end of the war a large number had been modified with increasingly sophisticated conversions; some of the later ones were equipped to carry aircraft. These ships found their most successful role with the 10th Cruiser Squadron on the Northern Patrol, ceaselessly searching the waters between Greenland, Iceland, the Faeroes, Scotland and Scandinavia for enemy blockade-runners. Medium sized passenger/cargo carriers, initially armed with eight 4.7-inch guns, were found to be ideal for the task, much better in the stormy, northern waters than regular cruisers which were, in any case, more profitably employed with the battle fleet. By the end of 1917 the Patrol had located and intercepted 8905 ships, 1816 of which were taken to port for inspection by ocean boarding vessels. The cost was high: there

were never more than twenty-five AMCs in the Squadron at any one time but seventeen were lost, twelve of them being torpedoed and two mined.

German raiders were not deployed in the numbers feared before the war but several were intercepted by AMCs and some significant ship-versus-ship actions resulted. On 14 September 1914 the *Carmania* with eight 4.7-inch guns sank the German *Cap Trafalgar* but was left seriously on fire, showing the vulnerability of these ships. On 29 February 1916 the *Alcantara* fought the German *Greif*, an action that resulted in both ships being sunk. The German ship was known to have been armed with 5.9-inch guns and so, as a result of this action, all British AMCs were re-armed with eight 6-inch guns and better watertight sub-division. As the war progressed, many AMCs were diverted to other duties and the 10th Cruiser Squadron was paid off in December 1917.

SLR1410 *Andes,* a sister-ship of *Alcantara,* was launched for the Royal Mail Line's South American service in 1913 and taken up from trade as an armed merchant cruiser in 1914. Like all AMCs she flew the White Ensign and she served with the 10th Cruiser squadron in the Northern Patrol until 1917 when she was used on convoy escort duty but reverted to mercantile service after the war, initially as a liner between Southampton and the River Plate and later as a cruise ship. This 1/96 scale model shows her after 1939 when she was taken up from trade for the second time and converted for duty as a hospital ship, renamed *Atlantis.* She survived her second conflict and returned to mercantile use; this time as an emigrant ship chartered by the New Zealand Government to carry migrants from the UK to New Zealand. She was not finally broken up until 1952.

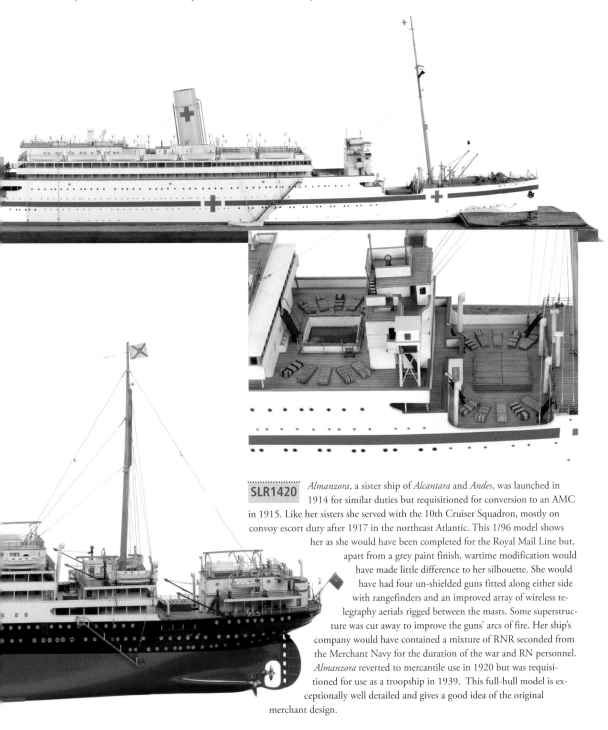

SLR1420 *Almanzora,* a sister ship of *Alcantara* and *Andes,* was launched in 1914 for similar duties but requisitioned for conversion to an AMC in 1915. Like her sisters she served with the 10th Cruiser Squadron, mostly on convoy escort duty after 1917 in the northeast Atlantic. This 1/96 model shows her as she would have been completed for the Royal Mail Line but, apart from a grey paint finish, wartime modification would have made little difference to her silhouette. She would have had four un-shielded guns fitted along either side with rangefinders and an improved array of wireless telegraphy aerials rigged between the masts. Some superstructure was cut away to improve the guns' arcs of fire. Her ship's company would have contained a mixture of RNR seconded from the Merchant Navy for the duration of the war and RN personnel. *Almanzora* reverted to mercantile use in 1920 but was requisitioned for use as a troopship in 1939. This full-hull model is exceptionally well detailed and gives a good idea of the original merchant design.

WAR STANDARD MERCHANTMEN

The Royal Navy maintained the free use of the oceans for Allied shipping throughout the war but the German U-boat campaigns, especially that of 1917, took a severe toll of merchant shipping. As part of the counter to this offensive, British shipyards built 'war standard' merchant ships to simplified designs quickly and efficiently, the new ships replacing losses on a scale that the enemy was unable to stem. One of the smaller patterns, the 'D' type were 'break-bulk', single-shaft cargo ships with reciprocating steam machinery – essentially large colliers – and were designed for mass production by S P Austin & Sons of Sunderland. All were given two-word names beginning with 'War' ranging from *War Acacia* to *War Zinnia* by late 1917. They were equipped with a single 4.7-inch gun aft for defence against U-boats on the surface that attacked with a gun rather than a torpedo and had fittings for paravanes to counter mines forward. Despite the defensive armament, they were always merchant ships flying the Red Ensign and can be considered the 'workhorses' of the world's oceans, forming an important, but often overlooked, element of Allied victory in 1918.

SLR1439 A finely detailed 1/96 scale model of *War Arrow*. She has four holds with king-posts between the forward and after pairs to work derricks that allowed her to unload cargo onto a jetty or into a lighter without the need for shore-side cranes. This was an important consideration which meant that there were few limitations to the number and variety of ports these ships could use. The derrick falls were worked by steam-powered winches on the upper deck sited near the bases of the king-posts. The single 4.7-inch gun is clearly visible on the poop deck aft where it had a wide arc of fire. It was manned by a defensively-equipped merchant ship party and was aimed over open sights using fixed ammunition provided from ready-use lockers by hand. The single screw and unbalanced rudder show the basic simplicity of the design. The fittings are gold-plated to make them stand out and the detailing in the central superstructure, including the bridge and lifeboats turned-in on radial davits, is superb.

SLR1433 This interesting model represents a group of 'break-bulk' cargo steamers built in 1915 by the Goole Shipbuilding and Repair Company and the Dundee Shipbuilding Company under Admiralty contract. They were operated by civilian crews but carried military stores ranging from ammunition to fodder for horses for the British Expeditionary Force across the English Channel. The ships were not given names but identified with a letter-number combination beginning with *A 24* and ending with *A 32*. This model was intended to show the generic design rather than an individual ship. They were austere, lacking all but the most important equipment and they were controlled from a small space just aft of the forecastle and forward of the first cargo hatch; a gold-plated ship's wheel can be seen there, together with a compass binnacle. The boiler and simple, reciprocating steam machinery were positioned right aft and this full hull model shows a single propeller and simple rudder. The ventilators that provided air to the single boiler are also gold-plated and just aft of the funnel. A small dinghy doubled as a lifeboat and is stowed on the after cargo hatch, from where it could be lifted into the water by the port after derrick. The four derricks are attached to the central king-post and were worked by the steam windlasses which can be seen to port and starboard; they, too, have been gold plated so that they stand out.

Further Reading

The warships that equipped the Royal Navy between 1914 and 1918 were the result of a fascinating period of development and change. Readers whose interest in them has been stimulated by this small book can find a great deal more information about the ships themselves, their armament and how to make models of them in other books available from Seaforth Publishing and the Naval Institute Press.

SHIPS

A wealth of information about battleships and battlecruisers can be found in the new and revised edition of *Battleships of World War One* by R A Burt which was published in 2012. Cruisers are described in Norman Friedman's *British Cruisers: Two World Wars and After* published in 2010, while some of the earlier ships that survived into the war years are covered in his companion volume *British Cruisers of the Victorian Era* (2012). The same author describes destroyers in *British Destroyers: From Earliest Days to the Second World War* published in 2009 and my own *British Aircraft Carriers* (2013) describes the aircraft-carrying vessels operated in the First World War as well as every subsequent development. Monitors are described in Ian Buxton's *Big Gun Monitors* re-published in paperback form in 2012 and the design of all types of British warship during this period are covered in D K Brown's authoritative *The Grand Fleet*, which was re-published in 2010 in a paperback edition.

WEAPONS

Both British and foreign weapons are described in Norman Friedman's *Naval Weapons of World War One: Guns, Torpedoes, Mines and ASW Weapons of all Nations* published in 2011 in which the sheer number of British entries shows how far ahead of others the Royal Navy really was. The development of big guns and their fire control systems is explained in *Naval Firepower* by Norman Friedman published in 2008, while the same author's *Naval Anti-Aircraft Guns & Gunnery* (2013) does a similar job for early anti-aircraft systems.

MODELS

The ShipCraft series covers a number of ship models but those specific to the First World War include *Grand Fleet Battlecruisers* by Steve Backer and *Queen Elizabeth Class Battleships* by Les Brown. *Thunderer* by William Mowll published in 2010 gives a fascinating insight into the making of a model of the last battleship to be built on the Thames, possibly the best model of a British battleship ever made. For those who have had their enthusiasm stimulated to the point where they would like to make their own model of a First World War ship, *Waterline Warships* by Philip Reed published in 2010 covers a warship from a later generation but gives valuable insight into the tools and techniques that would be required for any model. New books are being published all the time and readers are recommended to check www.seaforthpublishing.com and www.usni.org for details.